Let Me Speak to the Manager!

Avant® Leadership
Guide Series

Let Me Speak to the Manager!

Selling From the Buyer's Point of View

Daniel M. Boland, Ph.D.

Avant Books®
San Marcos, California

Library of Congress Cataloging-in-Publication

Boland, Daniel M.
Let me speak to the manager! : selling from
the buyer's point of view
Avant leadership guide series
1. Sales management. 2. Customer service.
3. Sales executives. 4. Executive ability. 5. Leadership.
HF5438.4.B65   1991   658.8'1—dc20   90-26716

ISBN 0-932238-57-2

Avant Books®
Slawson Communications, Inc
San Marcos, CA 92069-1436

Printed in the United States

Interior Design by Sandra Mewshaw
Art by Estay Heustis

1 2 3 4 5 6 7 8 9 10

Table of Contents

Chapter 1

What's the Problem?

It's often said that selling is an art. The artistic component is not simply the salesperson's ability to convince, persuade or manipulate the consumer. The art of selling is truly a human relations skill, its foundation is the manager's service mentality. Oddly enough, the goal of selling is not always a sale. A reputation for superior service is equally valuable for repeat business and referrals. The ultimate criteria are not just profits, but how well the salesperson treats the customer and how regularly the customer returns.

When it comes to sales, nothing happens by accident. A chain of interdependent events begins with the manager's service mentality and culminates in superior customer service. The salesperson is not an independent agent; he or she is a critical link in this service chain. Yet he is the first—often the only—personal representative customers encounter. His attitudes and behavior reflect the values and sensitivities of management. He sends a critical message to the customer: *You're respected or you're not.* Once it's sent, the message is irretrievably etched into the customer's mind.

The manager's influence and concern for service are the keys to selling from the buyer's point of view—and every customer knows it. In the long run, the customer reaps what the manager sows. That's why when things go wrong the customer will rightly proclaim, "Let me speak to the manager!"

Here's a brief example. At one time, my wife and I began each day at a little sidewalk cafe near our home. Hot rolls and freshly-brewed coffee made up for erratic, often surly, service. Despite the occasional rudeness of the manager and the indifference of his staff, we still returned frequently.

One morning I went inside to pay our bill. The manager was just a few feet away, reading his newspaper. The waiters were joking with the cook. All of them saw me, but none paid any attention. I waited. After several minutes the manager finally folded the newspaper with a sigh, shuffled slowly to the cash register, and casually took my money without a word or a glance.

We haven't returned since. We found another coffee shop just down the street where the coffee, the rolls, and—most of all—the service, are far more satisfying.

Incidents like this are not rare. You've probably had a similar experience as a consumer, but how about as a manager? Have you ever walked in on a heated scene between a distressed customer and one of your employees and heard the customer say in exasperation, "Let me speak to the manager!"?

That statement is the frustrated consumer's last resort, a final plea for service and satisfaction. When one of your customers asks to speak to the manager, your business is on the line and your reputation is at risk. If you don't handle the situation sensitively, it's all downhill from there. Once a dissatisfied customer starts repeating the incident to family and friends—and they always will—you can forget about repeat business and referrals. And there's no telling how badly that customer will embellish the story or how they'll maul your reputation in the telling.

The key to avoiding such unpleasant events is, of course, to make sure they don't occur. Your best resources are competent salespeople whose mission is to serve the customer *from the buyer's point of view*. Sometimes the superior service means no immediate sale in favor of a long-term relationship.

Many salespeople, even experienced ones, make two essential mistakes:

1. They try to *persuade*, instead of *listening*. In order to relate to customers' concerns, it is necessary to understand what those concerns are. When salespeople attempt to *sell a product* rather than *meet a need*, customers can quickly sense the true nature of the sellers' priorities.

2. If the customer wants to buy, he will. He may not buy from the salesperson, but the choice to buy is in the customer's hands. So, in most cases, the salesperson cannot talk a customer into buying, but she can talk the customer *out* of buying *from her*!

The two most important factors in long-term sales are keeping existing customers and enlisting new ones. To build a stable customer base, the manager will emphasize the Three Rs with salespeople:

Respect, Response, and Relationship.

1. **Respect:** Respect is a four-lane highway, not just a two-way street. Respect for customers begins with the manager's respect for his sales personnel. If the manager expects customers to be treated decently, he will realize that his first customers are his own employees. The manager's role is to cultivate the well-being and respect of workers. Then, and only then, can the manager and his business expect employees to work genuinely and consistently for the well-being and respect of the consumer.

For better or worse, customers eventually reap the harvest the managers sow with their employees. Managers prove by their own service-example that respect is a vital ingredient and a way of life in business, not just a shallow sales ploy.

2. **Response:** An effective manager is available to employees; not simply in terms of time but also in terms of support and attention. Many managers avoid involvement and keep their distance with employees. They respond only to technical foul-ups or discipline problems and have little else to do with their workers. They're good at managing technical matters, but not very good at leading people. Their aloof efficiency results in a lackluster work force and dispirited morale.

3. **Relationship:** Each brief contact between a manager and an employee contributes to a relationship between them. Each brief contact is loaded with emotional nuances and undercurrents, with

subtle signals and muted messages. These contacts also reveal the manager's hierarchy of values. The extent of her concern for her employees and for superior service are soon clear. Eventually the manager proves herself to be either authentic and supportive or contradictory and unreliable.

The effective managers preach what they practice: service comes first, even if it requires personal sacrifice. They encourage employees to express their doubts and reconcile their uncertainties. In some instances managers may act as *counselors*, helping employees clarify confusion and solve work-related problems in a confidential context. In other cases, an employee may call the manager's bluff; sometimes the manager may have to face his or her own contrary practices and swallow humble pie.

Egos and emotions are always involved on both sides of the manager-employee relationship. This also holds true in every sales exchange. The buyer's trust and the seller's credibility are part of every transaction. But in the long-run, a satisfactory sales relationship starts with the manager. It's the manager's example that sets the service mentality. The manager's credibility makes a significant difference in the quality and consistency of every employee's performance.

It is true that sales training is valuable. Training provides salespeople with standardized routines that managers monitor and coordinate. Training also provides the technical guidelines that make life easier for managers; ambiguity and risk are minimal. But most training is designed for the convenience of the bookkeeper or the computer, not for the salespeople or their customers. And most training is tedious and sterile, there's not much room for employees to improvise. Little is left to their initiative, intuition, inspiration or imagination.

By itself then, training is simply not sufficient to convince employees that the service mentality comes first. More is needed. An effective sales force requires the constant inspiration and energy of the manager's leadership. By the constancy of his leadership and the generosity of his example, the manager impels employees to superior service. His leadership evokes initiative and commitment in employees, not just routine compliance and cautious obedience.

It's not enough that the manager is occasionally considerate or generally fair. Employees trust and accept only what they can anticipate. Occasional support or sporadic courtesy breeds a tentative, walk-on-eggshells environment. Trust in the manager is rarely present when unpredictability is the norm. Like it or not, the burden of credibility and consistency rests first and foremost with the manager. Certainly employees must cooperate, motivate themselves and give their best—but that can take time. The manager must patiently lead the way, perhaps for a long, tedious time. That's why leadership often requires personal virtue as well as managerial know-how.

The manager's credibility also involves trust that is not quickly granted nor easily earned. Americans no longer give blanket credibility to anyone in business, not even the boss. What are some of the leadership qualities that merit respect and confidence from employees?

- Honesty: Is the manager ethical or does she cut corners? Is she sensitive to the finer points of moral behavior? Is she aware of her impact on people? Does she abuse power? Does she stretch the truth or deliberately lie? Does she mislead in minor ways? Does she exaggerate or make promises which she then ignores? Is she artificially sincere and easily distracted? Does she keep her word? Is she loyal to her employees as well as the company? What sort of example does she set? Is she an example of the service mentality?

- Responsiveness: Is the manager's word truly his bond? Does he care what employees feel and think? Is he concerned about morale? Does he take pains to be available to employees? Does he trust employees? Does he make reasonable allowances? Is he supportive and not harsh, or unnecessarily critical? Does he listen attentively or is he abrupt and interruptive? Does he invite open, frank communication? Can he confront without intimidating?

- Predictability: Is the manager in competition with employees? Is she dependable or does she vacillate? What's her track record? Does she come through consistently? Is she reliable or reckless? Does she demonstrate a sense of prudence, justice, and fairness? Is she emotionally stable? Does she play favorites? Is she erratic? Does she hold grudges or reveal confidences? Does she have mood swings?

- Competency: Is he a professional? Does he know the business? Does his ego get in an employee's way? Does he know what he's doing? Does he do his homework? Does he get the facts, or merely shoot from the hip? Is he informed and current or does he live in the past? Is his judgment good? Can he admit his mistakes? Does he seek advice when he's in doubt? Is he complacent? Is he motivated? Does he take credit for other people's success? Does he learn from employees?

A manager's credibility is built upon a combination of knowledge, technical competence, and psychological acuity, experience, and integrity. One way of checking your own credibility is to ask yourself the following questions, or better still, ask a colleague you trust to give some personal feedback.

Manager Credibility Check List

√   Am I rigid or flexible with employees?

√   Do I listen to employee concerns and take time to find out what they are?

√   Can I be trusted to do what I say, even in little things?

√   How much am I willing to learn? And from whom?

√   What good qualities do I bring to my work that rub off on employees?

√   Do I intimidate people or offer my genuine support?

√   Am I self-centered, or do I show concern for others?

√   How quickly do I stop trying to communicate with an employee, then rationalize or become righteous about it?

√   Am I hostile or supportive?

√ When is the last time I asked an employee or colleague, "Is there anything I can do to help you do your job more efficiently? What can I do to help?"

√ Am I cold and aloof or do I have a spirit of openness?

√ Am I apathetic or authentically committed in attitude and action?

√ Am I emotionally brittle and unpredictable, driving employees away or making them tiptoe around me?

√ Do I acknowledge employees who are obviously involved and competent (even if I do not particularly like them), or do I play favorites?

√ Do I have the sensitivity of an honest leader or just the arrogance of the defensive, egotistical pretender?

√ Do I acknowledge an employee's good work openly, without faking it? Do I offer compliments to employees when deserved or do I consider this unnecessary ("They're getting paid, that's enough.")?

√ If I could change one thing about myself that would make me a better leader, what would it be?

√ What prevents me from making that change—starting today?

√ What ego-need of mine gets in my way and in the way of employees?

√ What do I need to motivate myself toward greater commitment and better leadership?

√ In what ways are employees treated better because of me?

√ In what ways can I help employees be more effective?

√ Is the employees' working environment better because I am their manager? If so, how? If not, how come?

√ Is it pleasant to work with me?

√   Am I sensitive about my language and courteous toward employees?

So, what's the real problem in the art of sales? Developing generous, consistent managers who believe that the service mentality is not a gimmick but a way of life that begins, not with customers, but with employees.

Chapter 2

What Managers Need to Know About Leadership

Managing effectively is demanding. The endless details, aggravations, responsibilities, and time-consuming trivia drain the manager's reserves. And there's an emotional price to pay; effective managers can't always express themselves as they would like. They must motivate employees, please customers, pursue profits, and prove themselves to *their* boss; often stifling real feelings, anger, and humor. They must be technical experts, career diplomats, quick decision-makers and part-time psychologists. Energy must be summoned when they're exhausted, ready answers must be given even when there are none, and they must be patient when they're ready to explode.

Why bother?

Some managers persevere because it's a good living. Others stick with it because they're on their way to the *Executive Suite*. Still others truly enjoy the art of managing people, it's what they choose to do. For them, managing is a vocation, not just a job. Their work is a highly rewarding part of their lives; they take great pride in being a manager. Their work leaves its imprint on their character and shapes their values. Their work is an expression of personal vision, a statement about their hopes and ideals.

Self-image and personal esteem are tied into what people do and how well they do it. Some people would be seriously handicapped without the challenges and the self-expression opportunities that work affords. Ask any experienced manager, he'll tell you his role and responsibilities have a profound influence on his outlook and way of life.

Still, today's manager daily faces a serious dilemma, keeping the human dimension in perspective. Maintaining concern and integrity, while competing effectively is far from easy. Headlines remind us daily how frail human nature is and how flaccid and brief human resolve can be.

As the organization's pre-eminent representative to employees and, through them to the customer, the manager is responsible for profits and cost-effective procedures. He wields power and control over people's lives. Sooner or later he's called upon to impose unpopular edicts and unilateral decisions. The temptation is to be blunt and abrupt—calling it management efficiency. The manager can become thorny, hard-nosed and head-strong, concerned about running the organization and controlling (but not respecting) its members. People-problems can easily become nothing but unwelcome distractions.

Moreover, modern management is an intricate and sophisticated science. Management skills have become distinct technical skills. They're not innate and are improved only through learning. Seat-of-the-pants, *good-ole-boy* management is a thing of the past. Managing is a high-pressure profession, it's typically not for the lazy or faint-hearted, nor for people upset by friction or contentious interactions. Given all of this, it's not surprising that many managers lose sight of people, and of the human dimension.

But the manager's dilemma has a solution. It lies in the ability to integrate the qualities of an effective leader into management endeavors. The manager's three biggest challenges are:

1.   To blend his or her technical skills and organizational power with the personal traits of responsive leadership,

2.   To translate leadership into a service mentality,

3. With the goal of helping employees sell from the buyer's point of view. Probably the toughest challenge is to integrate the talent of a leader with the task of a manager.

Management and leadership have been synonymous for a long time. In reality, they are separable functions, two distinctive (and not always complementary) ways of thinking and acting. They may require different—sometimes conflicting—attitudes and skills, not always found in the same person. Some individuals may be excellent managers, but not strong or credible leaders. Others may have leadership ability but may have difficulty in managing effectively. Of course, successful organizations need good management and effective leadership to survive, but they keep both functions in balance. They are neither overmanaged nor underled.

Leadership ability is not necessarily connected to the manager's role or automatically linked to the job, nor is it guaranteed simply by status. Leadership is related more to one's personal persuasiveness and moral influence than to one's power over others. Leadership credibility hinges more on personal traits, such as reliability, careful listening, telling the truth, and developing new and original ideas. A genuine leader infuses people with vitality, spirit and idealistic vision. At the same time, the complex nature of today's organizations often dictate that a leader's influence may be effective in only one sphere of activity, while highly limited in another. Many workers and organizations are run by clever managers who never really develop into authentic leaders.

What specifically does a leader do that differs from a manager's activity? Here are some examples. Most of the following differences hold true in practice, but there are areas that overlap. Each of these models—leadership contrasted with management—is valid in its particular sphere, yet each has a different, and quite profound, impact on the culture and spirit of the organization. Each model contains assumptions about management-employee relationships, about communication and performance.

Management is concerned with how an organization handles the complexities it invariably develops. Managers are concerned about the organization's overall goals and well-being. Managing embraces the technical functions that guide the institution through today's intricate maze of finance, marketing, tax laws, legal issues, personnel hassles, hiring, firing, retirement decisions, insurance, borrowing and lending policy, investment decisions, political issues, market expansion, even public relations and media affairs.

Management brings control, order, direction and consistency to the overall operation of the organization. Without effective management, every institution tends to get mired in its own maze, eventually veering off into chaos and, in all probability, bankruptcy.

Leadership, on the other hand, focuses on the well-being of individuals and small groups within the organization. It is concerned about helping people cope with change when—even before—it occurs. Change in our world is so fast and unexpected that adapting to it is less useful than anticipating or even creating it.

Other practical differences between management and leadership flow from these distinctions. The differences are not usually *either-or*. The manager must choose the appropriate approach and prudently match timing to varying situations and circumstances. Experience and judgment are most helpful. Some of the practical differences include:

- Managers view people in light of the organization's goals and purposes. Leaders are more concerned about how the organization can serve individuals.

- Managers rely on predictable structures, specific goals and step-by-step plans. Leaders tend to accept ambiguity and uncertainty; they often support risky experimentation and visionary idealism.

- Managers look at specific data, such as inventories, ledgers and accounts, profit-and-loss statements, tangible goods, billable services and orderly procedures. Leaders tend to accept intuition and inspiration which are often fuzzy, unstructured and disconcertingly vague. Leaders also focus more on *soft* issues like morale, emotions and community spirit.

- Managers usually motivate workers by contractual relationships, time-clock rewards, salary, advancement and fringe benefits, paid vacations, insurance allowances and sick leave. Leaders usually motivate less by external incentives, more by the compelling nature of their ideas, by the consistency of their example, and by the infectious energy of their commitment.

- Managers work from an institutional power base which customarily uses peer pressure, supervisory manipulation, on-the-job intimidation or legal restraints to control workers. Managers ordinarily make unilateral decisions, assign tasks and time-lines, and coordinate group efforts. Leaders exert interpersonal influence and moral persuasion. They tend to stimulate voluntary participation and accept spontaneity.

- Managers control behavior, standards, procedures and bottom-line results. Leaders resist the tendency to exert control, they even tend to share control or give it away. They are more concerned with originality and unfettered self-expression.

- Managers function within a closed system of rank, vested authority, status and hierarchical exclusivity. They acknowledge only select members of the community as their peers; others are seen as subordinates or outsiders; formal titles are commonly used. Managers also dislike open criticism and discourage uncensored feedback from subordinates. Leaders try to treat people as community consultants, colleagues or co-equals. They emphasize interdependence, equality, and inclusive community. They expect, even encourage, open communication and feedback.

- Managers control the flow of data and parcel out information, secrecy and restricted access are common. Leaders usually share as much as they can. When information is sensitive, confidentiality is expected.

- Managers coordinate sales-and-marketing, target various markets, and maintain customer relations. Leaders are less concerned with selling than they are with offering their employees an example of professionalism, commitment and idealism.

In short, an organizational leader provides a generous example to employees and colleagues—and even to the larger society. The leader willingly gives his energy and availability to employees, even when it is inconvenient and fatiguing.

His or her basic question is, "What path can I choose to make my organization a better place for my workers, even if it means giving up something of myself—my time, my ego, my comfort."

The leader's motto is, "Give more than expected, take less than allowed."

How do these differences appear in practice? The issue of institutional control is an example.

Some form of control over people's actions is central to all management. Control requires enforceable conformity. To protect conformity, management traditionally keeps individualism and criticism at a minimum. Uniformity in sales procedures, dress codes, standards of behavior, even a common idiom, are ways organizations exert control.

When deviation from an organizational norm occurs, corrective structures automatically move into action. Pre-determined measures are initiated for the *good of the organization*. Details may vary and names may change, but fail-safe survival procedures endure. Exceptions are rare and individuals are routinely disciplined or sacrificed with a degree of impersonality. The institution is served; management control is, for the most part, maintained.

While convenient for management, this method of exercising control may be harsh on individuals, repressive to small groups, and viewed as inappropriate by leaders who encourage responsible self-expression. Leaders want to unify people, not dominate them. They generally wish to share power rather than to centralize it, to remove controls rather than impose them. They believe that uniformity tends to diminish responsibility rather than energize it.

Understandably, many managers take serious issue with giving people so much leeway. Managers who dislike giving up power or the easing of controls, also find this model too uncomfortable and risky.

In addition, there are employees who simply do not respond well to openness and freedom. Some people fear too many choices; they are incapable of acting without structure and direction. There are others who view it as an opportunity to become inefficient and uncaring. Both types need to be managed more than led.

So the manager has an immense challenge: to exert leadership skills without losing sight of management responsibilities. It boils down to the treatment given employees; to those fleeting but immensely significant moments in which the manager's attitudes and sensibilities convey a message of service and concern for individuals. Whenever a manager deals with an employee, everything he says and does counts. Cumulatively, nothing is insignificant.

Eventually, everything contributes to a relationship between the manager and the employee. Everything either adds to, or detracts from, the quality of the work environment. One day, it all comes back to compliment or haunt the manager. And it won't stop there. In the long run—for better or worse—customers reap what the manager sows.

So, while managing means running the organization, leadership means giving employees an example of generous and inspired service. Service means helping employees sell from the buyer's point of view. This is the manager's first responsibility. It is also his leadership challenge.

Chapter 3

The Manager's Influence: Implementing the Service Mentality

The first principle of leadership in business is to serve, not dominate employees. For the manager seeking to exercise leadership with employees, the service mentality means giving more than expected while taking less than allowed. She or he leads by the persuasive examples of fairness, generosity and consistency.

Hard-nosed managers find this principle difficult to accept. They associate service with customers, not with employees; employees should do as they are told. These managers confuse forcefulness with effectiveness and service with servility. Forcefulness relates to the use of the manager's power to control employees. Effectiveness relates to moral influence. A true service mentality is rewarding; servility is demeaning. The manager's leadership challenge, then, is not to control but to inspire and concentrate the energy of the salesperson. If the manager is true to the service mandate, his leadership will be effective and persuasive; the salesperson cannot help but be influenced.

If, on the other hand, a manager is more intent on flaunting authority, exploiting status, and protecting perks, he or she is not acting as a reputable or credible leader. If the manager is unfair, takes employees for granted, uses a double standard, does not pull his or her share of the load, ignores employees, lies or is otherwise offensive and arrogant, morale and motivation are obviously at risk. Productivity will suffer, not because of the employees, but because the manager is not doing the job.

Productivity is more than just a measure of profits or sales quotas. It encompasses the employee's morale and motivation. Morale is the emotional context in which people perform. It's the collective spirit, the psychological atmosphere and moral energy that motivates people to want to produce. Productivity results from the fusion of motivation and morale. Productivity is a sign of how competent and how willing people are to produce. When competence and desire combine, positive morale results and productivity increases.

The manager's service mentality is central to morale and motivation, *you get from people what you give.* The service mentality works best in an atmosphere of civility and respect. These qualities are evident in the way employees speak about their work, the manager, and the customer. When the manager does not demonstrate an attitude of service, even the most idealistic salesperson will not indefinitely sustain courtesy. Every employee soon learns the manager's priorities and thereafter wastes little effort on pretense with customers. A hostile manager creates hostile employees who destroy customer relations. An indifferent manager begets indifferent salespeople who are careless about service. For better or worse, customers reap what the manager sows.

Today's employee is frequently skeptical of management's real intent. It can be quite difficult for a manager to prove sincerity about commitment to service; loyalty and trust do not come easy. A service mentality among managers is not common, particularly in institutions where management egos regularly collide. But leadership is never a 50-50 proposition anyway, so, despite the employees' resistance, the manager will persevere. In a service mentality, management *head games* must be avoided and there cannot be an aloof, ego-stroking mystique to confuse employees. They must be listened to attentively, and—most of all—they must be told the truth. Of all the leadership tasks facing managers, listening intently and telling the truth are probably the roughest and riskiest. At the same time, these are the tasks that most often produce appreciation in employees.

If the manager acts with consistency, integrity and conviction, the example will sooner or later develop a service mentality in the employees and in the organization.

How does the manager implement the service mentality? Twenty-five years of consulting experience suggest that the following procedures will make a significant positive difference:

- Helpful use of power: The effective manager gives directions clearly and as often as it takes. He or she is steady and even-handed with authority and doesn't make a big deal about it. Whenever asked, he is willing to explain reasons for decisions. He appeals to reason and understanding rather than servile obedience.

- Develops others: The manager gives constructive feedback, evaluates strengths and weaknesses objectively and seeks to improve his personal shortcomings by eliciting feedback from employees.

- Supportive delegation: Delegation is not a test of an employee's ability, but a share in the manager's authority. Authority is delegated so employees can provide extra service without undue dependency. People are allowed to do their jobs; information and resources are offered when needed.

- Clear standards: High standards are maintained but the manager remains flexible. Unless an employee is a problem, the manager's belief is maintained in the employee's ability to complete the job and improve performance. Teamwork and cooperation with other work groups is stressed. Credit for successes is shared. If an employee becomes a problem the matter is handled privately and confidentially. The manager never threatens.

- Self-confident: As a rule, the manager is assured and unhesitating, never dwelling on the past or lingering over decisions. When there is doubt, assistance is sought; and he or she never fakes competence. It is recognized that a lack of knowledge is not ignorance and that seeking help is a strength, not a weakness.

- Logical: Experience helps a manager see patterns and relationships. Speaking precisely is important if the manager's instructions are to be understood. Questions are solicited and explanations are offered as often as needed. A follow-up guarantees that instructions were understood.

- Emotionally open: The manager is available to listen, advise, and assist in decisions; but never to psychoanalyze, harshly criticize, or cynically belittle. A closed, withdrawn manager produces an unsure, suspicious, work force. The employee will assume, rightly or wrongly, that the coldness and aloofness are signs that distance is preferred. The salesperson will understandably minimize contact and keep a low profile.

On the other hand, the open manager must guard against favoritism, or getting too close to certain employees while avoiding or merely tolerating others. If unavailable for an employee meeting, the manager schedules a later appointment.

- Flexible: When possible, the manager is reasonable and accommodating. The spirit, as well as the letter of rules is respected. By-the-book managers tend to be rigid and inflexible; morale and self-motivation are soon stifled.

- Appropriately vulnerable: Neither defensive nor touchy, the manager does not spend time covering mistakes, pretending to be right, or denying that feedback and advice are often needed. She or he realizes that the best way to handle mistakes is to correct them at once, and that only an emotionally secure person is able to be vulnerable and comfortable at the same time. The defensive manager protects against criticism and plays it so safe that employees cannot make suggestions or try anything new. Worse, when thing go wrong, the defensive manager finds scapegoats to shift the blame.

- Sensitive: The manager's attitudes are visible in his actions. The employees continue to search for weakness in management's credibility and example. Nothing is neutral when it comes to the service mentality and building trust. The manager cannot be flippant with employees, and nicknames or last names are never used when addressing them.

Confidentiality is protected and caution is always used so an employee does not feel put down, even in jest. Personal questions are never asked and an employee is never criticized in front of others. In general, employees are treated the way the manager would like to be treated by the boss.

- Altruistic: Altruism does not mean blind allegiance to employees. But the manager is willing to attend to the well-being of employees, even when it's inconvenient. Morale is boosted significantly when employees can rely on generosity and support. The self-centered manager does not generate trust and loyalty. The employee is inspired to act just as the manager does: concerned mainly with personal needs.

- Patient: An impatient manager taps his fingers, shows agitation, rushes people's speech, looks around distractedly, and avoids others. Impatience begets frustration and leads to antagonism and anger. Angry employees do not perform well. They develop informal networks and self-righteous cliques in which unhealthy antagonism binds people together; griping flourishes and frustration simmers.

- Truly hearing: Many managers simply do not listen and never really hear employees. Listening intently is the clearest sign of caring. Probably the finest compliment an employee can make about a manager is "He really tries to listen and hear what I say."

Listening and hearing are enormously personal gifts. They are deliberate choices made for the well-being of the employee. By listening carefully, we say, *I value you enough to take my time and make a conscious effort to understand your experience and concerns.* Without effective listening and hearing, corporations dissolve; so do marriages. Attention and empathy are rare indeed, but their power is undeniable and convincing.

- Not personally critical: Certain management judgments are appropriate and inevitable. The manager must judge employee performance according to accepted standards. In some settings, that's valid, but there is a significant difference between criticizing job performance and criticizing individuals. Indiscriminate judgments about an employee's personality, values or character are entirely out of order. When harsh or critical judgments about a person's performance are called for, it must be in the strictest confidence. Even when an employee is wrong, he still has rights.

- Fair, predictable, and consistent: These are the most important qualities a manager can display, the *essential condition* in the art of leadership. There are two ways this can be illustrated: (1) Ask your employees (one at a time) what they really want from you as their manager; and, (2) look back in your own work life. What qualities in your past managers made your work difficult? What qualities made your work easy? Most work problems are caused by a manager who is unfair, unpredictable and inconsistent.

The surest measure of the manager's service mentality and leadership effectiveness is his answer to this question: "As a general practice, am I honestly using my power and personality for the best interests of my employees, or for my own personal gain?" If it's for personal gain, it's probably done at the expense of the employees. This, they will never forget, and will probably pass their resentment along to the customers. In the long run, customers reap what managers sow.

Finally, here are suggestions for effective leadership that managers in every profession can follow.

As a manager I should:

√   Be frank and honest, not punitive, with employees.

√   Maintain employees' interests as much as my own.

√   Listen carefully to employees' concerns before I speak.

√   Listen carefully to employees' intent as well as their words.

√   Come to each encounter more as a learner than a teacher, more as a
       listener than an expert.

√   Leave my ego at home.

√ Learn to help others on their terms.

√ Tell others how they can help—and then let them do it.

√ Give more than expected.

√ Take less than I am allowed.

√ Be willing to do what no one else is willing to do, and then keep my mouth shut once it is done.

√ Always respect and observe confidentiality, no matter how small the issue may appear to be. Issues may seem small, but people's feelings are always great.

√ Follow my own role models and ethical ideals so that I can be a role model and an ideal for those with whom I work.

Chapter 4

Leadership and the Ethics of Service

To be professional, one must first be ethical. The manager's credibility rests on ethical consistency. Ethics reveal true values, attitudes and beliefs. The ethics of service require justice and courtesy with customers and fairness and generosity with employees. It is not enough simply to avoid wrongdoing; leadership requires far more. The ethical manager does the morally generous thing—giving more than asked while taking less than allowed.

Not every manager is convinced of the usefulness or necessity of ethics. For some managers, having ethics simply means not getting caught cheating, lying, or short-changing customers. This is a nasty notion of ethics. It inspires employees to walk a moral tightrope, to get away with as much as possible, to duck or deny responsibility. It easily leads to irresponsibility, cutting corners, selling inferior merchandise, misrepresenting products, belittling competitors, making impossible promises, stealing clients, and a host of dishonorable deeds.

There are two main views of business ethics. One is a legalistic approach that observes the minimum one must do to avoid trouble. Ethics is a way of staying out of jail or avoiding bad publicity; doing the right thing is motivated by fear of outside forces, not personal integrity.

The other outlook seeks the well-being of people through a service mentality. It says society is really an interdependent community; one's actions affect many other people.

While law protects the customer against unethical businessmen, ethics inspires generosity and trust. Law is negative and cautionary; ethics is positive and provocative. Law defines wrongdoing and punishes deceptive behavior; ethics expands our options. Law protects and defends against abuse; ethics embodies altruistic ideals.

So let's be clear: The ethics of service demands more than simply avoiding crime and wrongdoing. It involves moral virtue and requires a sustained commitment to moral principles. The ethics of service is based on a respect for humanity; it includes responsiveness to the needs of others. It inspires us to honor moral values and maintain consistency between the means and the ends of our actions. It prompts us to risk our own self-interest for the sake of our moral values.

Ethics is not something we do; it's something we are. Ethics is character distilled. Because the ethics of service often contradicts the economics of unrestrained profit, the ethical manager needs a special vision. He needs a moral perspective which may indeed conflict with the attitudes and practices of others. Most managers *really do know* right from wrong. They recognize the ethical from the unethical, the morally generous from the selfish. Knowing right from wrong is not the hard part of ethics. The hard part is maintaining idealism, altruism, empathy and generosity. The hard part is keeping character and integrity intact, maintaining self-respect, going beyond the moral minimum, overcoming moral lethargy, and rising above the herd instinct. The hard part is facing the moral twists and turns that lurk in unquestioned profit. The hard part is giving more than required and taking less than allowed. The hard part is believing, despite the cynicism and contrary practices around us, that we are on the right track.

Ethical management is emotionally costly; it creates, rather than resolves, ambiguity. The ethical ideal—doing what is right and generous for employees and customers, even when we're not required to do so—can always be pushed a little bit further; there is always more that we can do to help others. The moral tug of ethics is constant, it asks a lot. It requires sacrifice and generosity for the accomplishment of its goals. But it is also contagious, living ethically and openly with nothing to hide is still the safest and least stressful way to live. As the late John Henry Faulk said, "The greatest relief and finest solace in life is doing the right thing, and knowing you're right."

But many managers understandably grow weary under pressure. They demand less of themselves, cut corners and wink at questionable tactics. Discouragement comes from a number of sources: lack of support, criticism from careless colleagues, unethical superiors, feelings of isolation, apprehension about job security, fear of retaliation, emotional burnout and spiritual tedium are but a few. But almost all the faults of an unethical manager are more pardonable than the methods used to obscure them.

In the long run, ethics is a significant part of all legitimate success. Sooner or later, every moral person must cope with the inconveniences of generous service and the irksome demands of ethical practice. Here are several ways the manager can stay afloat ethically:

• Select one ethical standard and live by it, no matter what price or pressure is involved. Decide never to compromise on this one principle. Be willing to pay a price for this conviction. Make it something you believe in and can practice, even when it is embarrassing. Start with little opportunities, build toward the goal of making it a habit. Stand for something. You do not have to be overbearing, arrogant or flaunting. But when the time comes, let people know you mean business. This is true leadership.

• Develop an altruistic spirit, a generous responsiveness to employees and customers. Altruism is an ethical trait which springs out of the service mentality. It involves giving to others without hooks and without expecting anything back, even if it costs something personal. The highest form of ethical action is altruistic behavior that asks nothing in return; not future favors, not even allegiance to creed, sect or political party. Even most churches do not practice such idealism.

• Focus your energies on developing beneficial contacts with employees and customers. Avoid pettiness, jealousy and conflict. Strive to help people, not wound them, nor arbitrarily pull rank. Traits such as trust and hope have beneficial effects on the human system. Cynicism and helplessness are associated with illness. Caring generously about others is good for our health.

• Remember, nothing is neutral in human affairs. In our contacts and relationships—whether brief or long-term—we work best when we approach people wanting the best for them, customers and employees alike. This means maintaining patient concern for people, despite their coldness, hostility or ignorance.

Ethics in business is a necessity, not a luxury. When called upon to make ethical decisions, here are some practical questions the manager can ask:

1. Will my decisions violate the trust, rights or good will of others?

2. What are the motives and spirit behind my actions, greed or legitimate profit?

3. If I cut corners, fudge, cheat or get away with something dubious, will it add to, or detract from, my reputation? If it adds to my reputation, perhaps I should wonder about my associates.

4. If I describe my decision in public tomorrow, will I do so with pride or shame?

5. How would it be received by people whose integrity I respect?

6. Even if my action is not illegal, is it done at someone else's personal expense? (For example, their trust in me, their reputation, or good will)?

7. Is my decision fair? Just? Morally right? Is it in the best interests of those affected?

8. If this was done to me, would I approve and agree, or would I take offense and be insulted?

9. What are the basic principles I use to conduct business and model my standards of morality?

10. When I am in doubt, to whom will I go to check my ethical judgments?

11. Do my decisions give others (my family included) reason to trust or distrust me?

12. Am I willing to take an ethical stand when it's called for? Am I willing to make my ethical beliefs public; not in a *holier-than-thou* manner, but in a way that makes it clear to colleagues, friends, and loved ones (including my children) what I stand for morally?

13. Do I truly live by my values in private life? For example, do I take a newspaper from a stack without paying? Or do I stretch moral limits beyond what is legitimate, just because *everyone else does it*, or *who's to know?*

14. Can I take legitimate pride in the ethical example I give my employees (and my children) or do I have to occasionally avoid their gaze or fumble for an excuse?

Ethics gives meaning to our routine business endeavors and endows our transactions with a significance they would not otherwise possess. Indeed, the ethics of service inspire altruism and mutual respect, the foundations of public order. From that point of view, ethical idealism is really quite practical and essential.

John Ruskin once said "The highest reward for a person's toil is not what they get for it, but what they become by it." Behaving ethically may not pay more, nor does it bring us corporate adulation. So where is the reward? Most often it is within ourselves. We are ethical because it is makes sense for human beings to be ethical; it reveals us at our personal best. Ethics is a key factor in the life-long process of becoming a person who lives by, and for, his ideals, a person for whom moral values and ethical integrity are as essential in private life as the rules he follows and the leadership he exercises in business.

Human beings function best when working in collaboration and peace with one another—and that's what business is all about. There is no more convincing example to employees and consumers than a manager whose life and work are a daily example of the ethics of service—giving more than asked, taking less than allowed.

Chapter 5

When Fear and Distrust Intrude

Some years ago David, a colleague of mine, was sent to manage his company's Asian operations. His work was arduous, the details endless, and the strain considerable. He had to adjust to a strange language, dusty living conditions and a troublesome cuisine. The bright spot in David's fifteen-hour work day was his before-bed shower. The anticipation of standing beneath a cascade of cold water kept him going through tedious meetings and obscure courtesies unknown to American managers. David soon learned how the simplest events could be the most rewarding.

One late evening, as he stepped out of his ornate marble shower vigorously toweling his hair, David heard the slightest rustling and sensed movement at his feet. As he looked down through the folds of the towel, his entire body froze; a large cobra slid languidly across the cool tiles, inches from his toes. Fear rooted him to the spot. The towel remained motionless on his head, not out of deliberate caution but from sheer, paralyzing terror. It was, he later told me, the peak moment of dread in his adult life.

The paralyzing intensity of his fear probably saved David's life in those precious seconds. But he could take no credit for acting intelligently. His decision to freeze was made on an instinctual level. He was simply doing what came naturally: reacting defensively to a life-threatening event. In this case, David's intense fear saved his life.

Our responses to fear run a gamut from being briefly startled by a loud noise to the white-knuckle terror of a near-collision in midair. We have many names for fear: dread, consternation, awe, fright, dismay, panic, alarm. They are all triggered by an overriding sense of a power which exceeds our own. Fear conjures up forces in our mind that threaten our well-being. Fear evokes a sense of someone—or something—ominous, stronger, more in control than we are. Fear looms as an enemy that is able to seriously harm us physically or injure our ego or reputation.

A major part of our fear is the mystery and uncertainty—the *what if*—surrounding it. We do not know what damage it might inflict upon us. We're not sure that we can overcome, contain or survive its ferocity or intensity. Fear can be so deeply real that we cannot control or account for its effect upon us. But those effects are clearly present, nonetheless. Our body tells us so.

Fear and threat are useful and life-saving—sometimes. As David learned, it's realistic to be afraid of a poisonous snake as it slithers close to you. But constant threat or prolonged anxiety is no way to live or work.

Threat and anxiety are almost always useless emotions. Their only value is that they alert us to dangers in our lives or organizations. Anxiety tells us that something is seriously wrong. The source of anxiety is not too difficult to identify. But if that source is beyond our control, anxiety can be terribly frustrating.

Threatened, anxious people who are plagued with dread and distrust are also psychologically and spiritually unhealthy. They are in no condition to work effectively, deal with customers or even represent a business. Effective businesses need healthy people because they:

1.   Are more efficient and involved in their work.

2.   Do not fear using their talents and resources.

3.   Openly express concern for the well-being of others.

4.   Have a generous spirit and freely give their best.

5.   Also know the rewards that come from giving their best.

6.   Are self-motivated and waste neither time nor resources.

7. Are highly productive.

8. Have spontaneous professionalism unsullied by anxiety.

9. Have contagious professionalism unsullied by anxiety.

10. Are loyal, and loyalty can't be bought.

In many organizations, people are fearful about the future, their reputations and advancement, about events that they generally cannot control.

But what if the fearful events never occur (as is most often the case)? Then their fear was based on false and distorted information. People who worry about what might happen, fill in the unknown with the worst possible scenarios.

Unrealized fears obviously have no basis in fact. They are merely the misgivings and rumors of anxious people. They are based on distortions, lack of information, hearsay, and misunderstanding, but they're still enormously powerful. They still create tensions severe enough to hamper productivity and tie workers in knots. In other words, fear and anxiety do not have to be factual to cause harm. They merely have to be real *to employees* to produce stress, tension, threat and eventually distrust.

Sometimes a manager deliberately creates fearful, threatening environments. As one manager put it, "Fear is a great way to keep workers on their toes and off their feed." But if a worker cannot trust his manager, if on-the-job distrust, anxiety, and self-defense are necessary ways of relating to the manager, then morale and motivation will surely wither and die. The longer fear and distrust last, the more severe the cost to employees. They become emotionally disturbed; productivity is quickly disabled.

Anxiety and distrust produce costly physical consequences. The body's delicately balanced mechanisms—the immune, skeletal-muscular, respiratory, cardiovascular and digestive systems—can be seriously affected by prolonged distrust. Medical symptoms such as ulcers, colitis, heart trouble, chronic fatigue, and lowered resistance very often result from on-the-job anxiety. Symptoms such as urinary and digestive problems, chronic infections, even skin rashes, result from tense and fearful work settings. And that's not all.

Medical problems are bad enough, but psychological symptoms also surface when people are subjected to habitual fear and distrust. Emotional difficulties do not always receive immediate attention from the manager for several reasons:

1. Managers are simply not trained to handle psychological problems which may signal deep-seated personality conflicts;

2. These on-the-job emotional problems may seem less important because they do not always require immediate hospitalization;

3. They are often chalked-up to temperament or to a *bad* day.

4. Many managers are intimidated by emotional issues; they carefully avoid mentioning feelings or personality problems to the employee. These are sensitive areas, awkward to discuss and resolve without putting the employee on the defensive, making matters worse.

    Fear and anxiety have troubling affects on an employee's judgment, attitudes and actions. They jeopardize more than an occasional sale. They compromise the employee's competence and reliability. They endanger the business' reputation. They create friction with colleagues and bad will with customers.

Many changes occur in employees' thinking and behavior when they try to live with fear and adjust to constant distrust. Among the major changes are:

1. **The magnification effect:**

    Normal situations become blown out of proportion, small issues loom much larger than they really are. Innocent comments take on distorted meaning, small events become large ones.

2. **Reduced rationality:**

    The employee's thinking becomes clouded; he or she can become defensive and argumentative, saying and doing crazy, *off-the-wall* things.

3. **Reduced feelings of self-control:**

   As pressure mounts, a sense of losing control seeps in. Some people actually lose their grip on reality and may fly off the handle in an instant for no reason at all.

4. **Reduced memory:**

   Sometimes an employee under pressure forgets simple tasks or the names of associates and customers, often losing things or forgetting meetings. Accountability is severely diminished.

5. **Reduced performance ability:**

   There's diminished ability to accomplish one's work. The more anxiety, the less ability to perform efficiently. Driving a car when people are fearful or anxious is dangerous.

6. **Reduced tolerance:**

   The longer distrust lasts, the more patience and acceptance diminish until the employee is close to the emotional edge.

7. **Loss of self-awareness:**

   Some people experience a loss of self-awareness. This results in attacks of irresponsible behavior and feelings of rootlessness and diminishing commitment. They say, "I'm not myself today," or "I really forgot myself."

8. **The cumulative effect:**

   No single event sets people off, it's one thing after another. The increasing weight of pressures and strain eventually adds the last straw. Pressure becomes unbearable.

9. **The back burner effect:**

   If the fear or tension cannot be resolved right away, the employee will file them in the back of his or her mind and try to go on with the job. But these concerns cannot be completely stifled. They will simmer and create negative energy which, sooner or later, must vent itself in some sort of explosion.

10. **Hot talk:**

The back burner effect ignites an anxious dialogue. This hot talk feeds the employee's fear and keeps distrust alive. Even when the source is absent, anxiety can still be fresh and potent because its source is now within the employee, not outside. Hot talk fans the flames of distrust. The employee worries and rehashes threatening events.

With all the above changes occurring, it's no wonder morale slackens, motivation crumbles, absenteeism rises, decisions are avoided, meetings postponed, appointments missed, projects run at half-speed, communication stops, trust withers. The more distrust and anxiety an employee has to live with, the less effective he is. Anxious, distrustful people simply do not do their best work; sometimes they can't work at all.

Most managers are embarrassed to admit that fear exists in their organization. "Why should employees be afraid?" they ask. "There's no reason for fear or distrust here. We treat everyone fair-and-square. It's all in their minds, anyhow." At least that much is true, these psychological problems are indeed all in the employee's mind. That's exactly where they get their destructive power, from the mental and emotional energy generated by the employee's anxious thoughts and defensive emotions.

If the truth were known, the manager's statement would sound more like this, "I do not want to admit that I may be a threat to employees. There may be a lot going on under the surface I do not want to face. It makes me anxious to think that maybe—just maybe—I'm not effective." In other words, it's the manager's own fear that underlies the denial of fear in the organization.

When fear and anxiety do inhabit the workplace, the manager can only gradually reduce the employee's distrust. The process must start with empathy. The question empathy poses is not whether the employee distrusts the manager, but why? In practice, empathy means that the manager tries to see the employee's point of view, *as if* he or she is actually the employee.

The manager may not agree with the employee's outlook, but she needs to know what triggers the employee's fear and causes such distrust. The manager needs to know the attitudes and the things that threaten the employee. The manager needs to keep the following factors in mind:

1. The employee's perception is paramount. The threat arises from the employee's perception of danger as well as from reality. How much of a threat is the manager to the employee? What does the manager do that threatens the salesperson? There's one way to find out, ask.

2. It's the manager's responsibility. When it comes to building trust, the burden of proof is on the manager. Personal feelings may have to come second. This may seem one-sided, even unfair; it often is. But building trust starts when the employee no longer fears the manager.

3. How emotionally free are employees? Can the employee express an opinion before tasks or projects are assigned? Is he or she free to express ideas without retaliation? Is it possible to be direct and honest without incurring the manager's displeasure? Does the employee feel free to ask the manager to reconsider decisions?

4. How open is the manager? Is there an apparent willingness to talk things over? One manager recently mentioned that everyone in the office knew that he was about to ruin a project and lose a client, yet no one gave a warning. He later learned people were hesitant to speak up because he never indicated a willingness to listen to anyone. As a manager he did all the talking. He was caught off guard in the worst way; he lost the client and then his job.

5. Does the manager respect the employee? How often are honest compliments, positive feedback, or praiseworthy evaluations given? Does the employee receive credit for contributions or does the manager take it all.

6. How safe is the environment? Can the employee discuss a personal problem which affects her work? Can she trust the manager's judgment and rely on confidentiality? Does the employee feel that

suggestions are considered or does the manager jump right in with "If I were you . . ."?

Some amount of apprehension is present in every work environment. The trick is to keep fear and anxiety in balance and respect them for what they are: valid and valuable warning signals. Once fear and distrust are present, it is time to heed the warning and deal directly with their causes—even if fear temporarily heightens as a result. Anxiety intensifies as its source is approached. But the more the source is exposed, confronted and jointly handled, the less power it has to dominate people and defeat organizations.

Building trust and maintaining healthy work environments starts when the employee does not fear the manager. The ultimate danger of ignoring fear and distrust is that employees will be emotionally incapable of doing their jobs. In the long haul, fear will sap energy and commitment. No one is immune from the long-term ravages of fear: not management, not workers, not even customers.

A final comment, perhaps the manager's best approach to reducing distrust is a consistent service mentality. The service mentality prompts the manager (1) To listen intently to the employee's concerns; (2) To tell the employee the truth; (3) To remain vulnerably open while seeking honest feedback; (4) To be willing to give more and take less of what is allowed; and (5) To be patient while the employee takes time—perhaps months—to lower defenses.

Fear is an awesome adversary. It kills trust, communication, and the simple joy of achievement. Fear, distrust and anxiety stifle superior service and demoralize the spirit of all employees—including the manager!

Chapter 6

Developing Service Attitudes

Our attitudes are mixed packages of feelings and facts, emotional and mental medleys consisting of various beliefs, assumptions and perceptions. They are really convenient summaries of a wide range of subjects: work, politics, and religion, to mention only a few. Since our attitudes are taught, not inherited, they can change throughout life; we can indeed be profoundly influenced through example and education.

Our attitudes will vary with circumstances and people. For example, we'll react differently with children than with colleagues. A waiter will not receive the same treatment as a client. Our attitudes prompt us to censor words and actions, according to changing situations and relationships.

Our earliest attitudes (toward religion, for example) originated with our parents and are stored deep within our unconscious mind. But no matter how hidden or well-disguised they may be, these attitudes will still find expression sooner or later. Even with an arsenal of deceptive maneuvers, our attitudes will eventually show up in our actions.

For better or worse, this also applies to sales. For example, imagine a distracted salesperson lightly drumming his fingers and sighing (ever-so-slightly) while the customer studies several items. It does not take a psychologist to recognize that the salesperson reveals a host of attitudes about the job, the art of selling, sensitivity toward customers, and—most of all—about personal self-esteem. If the salesperson's manager is also impatient with customers or indifferent about service, the consumer will bear the brunt somewhere along the line. Indeed, many customers encounter such management attitudes in indirect, petty, and quite unexpected ways.

Here's a personal example, years ago I went to a movie matinee. I bought a seventy-five cent box of popcorn and settled in. When I took a few bites of the popcorn, I found it was stale, hard and greasy. I went back to the concession stand and asked for a replacement. The young man behind the counter was stunned at my request. He said he could not replace popcorn on his own authority and called the head usher for help. The head usher was also stricken with disbelief and said he too could not replace the popcorn.

"Let me speak to the manager," I requested. The manager turned out to be a surly, hostile man. His shirt was soiled and coffee-stained, his shoes scuffed and dirty. Without a handshake or smile he growled, "What's the problem?"

When I told him my stale popcorn story, he said they used only the best corn and quality oil to make the popcorn. I told him I did not question the quality of his raw materials; all I wanted, I said (my voice quivering and rising ever-so-slightly by now), was a replacement for a spoiled and inferior product. At this point he reached, uninvited, into my box of stale popcorn and helped himself to a greasy handful. As he munched, he said, "Tastes okay to me." Then he took the box from me and offered some to the head usher who said (not surprisingly), "Tastes okay to me, too."

My frustration increased, I was clearly getting nowhere so I asked the manager how I could contact his boss. After an argument and many offensive comments, he finally gave me the phone number of the theater chain's corporate headquarters in a distant city.

The next morning I called. After wading through several abrupt employees I finally reached the executive vice-president. He too was arrogant and challenging and I knew the outcome as soon as I heard his tone.

After several insulting minutes, I asked how I might reach *his* boss. "He's retired and living in Florida," he said. "I run the company now. If you want to write a complaint letter, send it to me."

"Will you forward it?" I asked.

"Not on your life," he answered.

A seventy-five cent box of popcorn eventually revealed how the attitude of top management filtered down to a teenage concessionaire selling stale popcorn a thousand miles away.

The manager's attitudes and examples have everything to do with an employee's attitude toward customers and the kind of service a client receives. If a manager is cynical, indifferent, or casual about meeting the customer's needs, the employees will also present this hostile attitude.

Here are characteristics about negative attitudes that every manager ought to know:

1.   They are always learned from someone else—usually older, more experienced people—no one is born with them.

2.   They are usually founded on half-truths and distortions; selfishness is usually at the core.

3.   Negative attitudes eventually show up in the employee's indifference toward the job and toward customers.

4.   Rumors, grudges, gripes, and hearsay are allies of negative attitudes. Truth is the best prevention.

5.   The most dangerous negative attitudes are those fed by cynical and insensitive managers.

6.   Disgruntled employees latch onto negative attitudes more quickly and firmly than positive ones.

7.   The more a negative attitude is expressed through griping, the more power and credibility it gains and the more contagious it becomes.

8.   If half-truths are the source of a negative attitude, constructive change will never occur unless the half-truths are confronted quickly.

9.   Negative attitudes always have a depressing affect on those who spread them and those who absorb them. Morale is always hurt.

10. They erode motivation, lessen productivity, contribute to depression and poor emotional and physical health.

11. They also contribute to job burnout.

12. They are different from legitimate gripes that can be useful when they're expressed without hostility, then attended to, defused and remedied.

13. An employee must be confronted immediately when a negative attitude is revealed in a salesperson's speech and action toward a customer. Do not let a day end without getting the matter resolved.

14. Customers remember the negatives with great resentment; far longer than they remember courtesy and good service.

15. Customers repeat bad experiences several times to other people; referrals always suffer.

16. Negative attitudes also spill over and affect home and personal life.

What can the manager do about negative attitudes? It's obviously better to develop positive attitudes. How? Several principles may help.

Principle #1—Relationships between managers and employees produce either positive or negative attitudes; there's no in-between. Since the manager has the power to form attitudes, his example is the lasting one. In the long run, the manager's example sets the tone for the salesperson.

Principle #2—Negative attitudes are best dealt with head-on, as soon as they appear. Employees with negative attitudes expect, then find, the worst. One way the manager can prevent negative attitudes from developing is to use a *prefer* rather than a *demand* approach. The *Prefer Approach* relies on discussion, negotiation, consideration of alternatives and mutual decisions. The *Demand Approach* is unilateral; it relies on imposed decisions, one-way communication and no negotiation about alternatives.

The *Demand Approach* may give a manager a sense of forcefulness and a rush of power. But it is seldom effective in the long-term.

Principle #3—Since the manager is constantly in the psychological limelight, she communicates some sort of attitude all the time, even when she is unaware that it is happening. Her example is subtle but constant. The manager communicates in three basic ways:

a. **Verbal communication:** this refers to spoken and written words that convey factual meaning;

b. **Non-verbal communication:** this refers to hand movements, head and body gestures, eye movements, facial expressions, posture, etc. that convey spontaneous emotional meaning;

c. **Meta-verbal communication:** this applies to voice pitch and tone, intonations and rhythms, grunts and sounds that add subtle emphases to words. Of themselves meta-verbal expressions may mean nothing; they make sense only in a specific situation or a particular context.

Principle #4—In most situations, problems result not from the content of the manager's message but from her style of communication. In other words, it's not simply what the manager says, but how she says it, that counts.

Content refers to the meaning of the words, to the sum-and-substance of the message. Style means the way the manager imbues her words with subtle nuances that add meaning. Style expresses a deeper emotional message tucked into the words. Sometimes its a pleasant and playful message, sometimes it's insulting and degrading.

Most problems relate to the *way* the manager says things to an employee. Is she being snide? Insulting? Sincere? Sarcastic? Sympathetic? Conflict almost always results from the manager's style and in the feelings which result.

Principle #5—To build positive attitudes, the manager has several demanding roles:

a. The manager is a model of healthy attitudes; he sets the example even at some personal sacrifice.

b. He is a problem-solver, not problem-maker.

c. He is the employee's main source of immediate support in the system.

d. The manager is the ethical leader in his part of the organization.

e. He is the trend-setter with his employees.

f. The manager is the catalyst in the system.

g. He is also the main source of clear and useful feedback.

Here are some suggestions for eradicating negative attitudes and building positive ones. These suggestions are basic to the manager's service mentality—giving more than asked, taking less than allowed. Negative attitudes are always founded on half-truth and distortion, so it is important for the manager to:

1. Dispel misinformation; tell the truth even if it is embarrassing.

2. Answer questions directly, if only to say, "I cannot answer that."

3. Explain minimum and maximum standards; ask each employee if he or she understands.

4. Communicate as often as necessary, never say, "I'm going to tell you this just once."

5. Allow the employee to make choices about his work whenever possible; regulate only when necessary.

6. Explain yourself to the employee, do not create ambiguity or uncertainty. Be approachable, emotionally stable and predictable.

7. Ask each employee—in private and one at a time—how you can help him do his job more productively.

8. Publish written performance standards long before evaluations.

9. Notice and comment on good performance—but never fake it.

10. Never talk about one employee to another.

11. Always respect confidentiality even when it does not seem needed.

12. Delegate by stating a preference, not demanding.

13. Always ask the employee if he or she understands what you are looking for and what you do not want.

14. Until you are proven wrong two times, assume that the employee has good will.

15. Watch your emotions; do not act defeated or show antagonism in front of an employee.

16. Do not encourage frustration by modeling it.

17. Never belittle or publicly criticize an employee.

18. As a rule, do not interrupt an employee when she's talking.

19. Acknowledge legitimate fears and gripes.

20. Do not speak for an employee or put words in his mouth; make sure you understand his point of view.

21. Do not lose your cool, especially in public.

22. Realize that most so-called problems are really inconveniences, so don't over-react or create disasters.

23. Don't arbitrarily defend or alibi yourself or the company; don't whitewash management's mistakes or belittle the employee's concerns.

24. Don't dwell on past performance, yours or the employee's.

25. You don't have to like an employee to work with him or her effectively, but you cannot demonstrate your dislike.

26. Everyone does not have to like you either.

27. When you have doubts, don't hesitate to get a professional opinion.

28. Managing people is not a 50-50 proposition; leaders lead out front, so take the first step before expecting the employee to follow.

29. Leadership demands that you lead, but not dominate.

30. You are, as a rule, responsible for the attitudes of your employees.

31. Employees also have a definite responsibility, hold them to it on a fair and consistent basis.

32. On a one-to-one basis, treat employees separately if similarly.

33. Never play games with an employee through excessive kidding, using a nickname, or trying to be a *good ole boy*.

34. When in doubt, ask, never presume.

Finally, as a general rule you get back from employees the kind of behavior, attitudes and loyalties you demonstrate. So do unto employees as you would have your manager do unto you!

Remember—you are the manager, your attitude is always showing.

Chapter 7

Delegating the Service Mentality

The manager cannot make every decision, employees need a degree of freedom. In those brief but critical moments with the customer, the employee should not be hampered by rules only the manager can interpret or change. The manager must give the employee some measure of authority to do the job in a clearly-defined manner. This is delegation.

Delegation grants more than a measure of management authority; it also invests the employee with responsibility for the attitude of service. Delegation encourages the salesperson to use his or her own judgment to assure superior service. There are a number of reasons for delegating authority:

1. It allows completion of a job which the manager might not finish alone.

2. The best people are selected and thereby competent resources are activated.

3. Deserving employees are given recognition and further motivation.

4. The energy of competent employees is released into productive directions.

5. Future management personnel are identified.

The sensible manager uses delegation to help the employee develop several significant traits: *(a)* self-esteem is always enhanced, *(b)* a sense of inclusion in the business is increased. *(c)* Feelings of control over work and career are bolstered; *(d)* The *What's in it for me?* factor is improved.

There are two kinds of delegation: (1) restricted delegation (the more common type), and (2) unrestricted delegation. Restricted delegation has limits and terms attached. That's fine as long as the employee knows the limits. Unrestricted delegation gives the employee free rein to make decisions. The employee has the same authority as the manager in specified areas, no hooks or reservations.

The manager also has the option of team or collective delegation. Teams extend delegation beyond a single individual. People tend to assume responsibility for what they do best. They gravitate to groups in which they are free to act. Collective delegation is a way of unleashing this self-selected talent that might otherwise remain untapped. With teams the manager needs to be consistent. Once team delegation is assigned and limits set, let team members make the choices.

Some managers dislike delegation and have a litany of reasons for not using it. They see it as a threat, a challenge or contest, not as a way to tap the employee's talent. They tell the employee, "Let's see what you can do," or "Let's find out how good you really are." This is a serious mistake, it's also unprofessional. Delegation isn't a test of the employee's ability, it's recognition that trust and confidence have been earned.

When resistant managers are compelled to delegate, their negative attitudes and restrictive actions can tie the employees into knots. The reluctant manager's tactics diminish the employee's freedom, stifle openness, and heighten defensiveness and resentment. The manager creates hostility, distrust, intimidation and poor morale by creating a *Catch-22* situation. Sometimes these management ploys are not deliberate, often they are. Either way, delegation and the employee's competence are undermined.

Here are examples of what *not* to do during the delegation process:

1. Since the employee should not have too much freedom, slap on rules and regulations.

2. Always compare one employee with another; keep them competing.

3. Keep checking on the employee to be sure no abuse of delegation exists.

4. Ask for daily reports; that keeps them on edge.

5. Define in great detail how the task should be done so the employee does not take too many liberties.

6. Bring up past failures to guard against failure now.

7. Use put-downs, negative language, and reminders of what will happen if there is a screw up.

8. Withhold positive feedback so that no big egos are created.

9. Give corrections in public; this will serve as an example and keep others on their toes.

10. Tell the employee, "It's your baby now, don't ask me," then, let the project get out of control so everyone will know who's the boss.

11. Change the terms of delegation in midstream; alter the focus frequently and manipulate the conditions unexpectedly.

12. Assign selfish motives to the employee's actions so no real trust can ever exist.

13. Give frequent advice; leaning over the employee's shoulder say, "What you ought to do is . . ." Allow no time for a personal style to develop.

14. Don't listen to the employee's ideas; tell her or him how to do everything.

15. Agree enthusiastically with whatever the employee says, even when you think it is wrong and off-base.

16. Withhold communication entirely. Let the employee go off on all sorts of tangents without answering questions or cautioning as to possible consequences.

17. Lock the employee into rigid patterns. Tie him to your way of doing things and holding to established procedures. Don't allow anything new or experimental.

18. Reveal surprise (real or fake) at the employee's decisions and actions. This causes self-doubt and builds dependence on you.

19. When feelings are expressed, belittle them by saying, "You really don't mean that," or "Everyone feels that way," or "We all have problems." Make the employee feel stupid for sharing his emotions.

20. Make snide comments, such as, "I know you think you are a hot-shot, so here's a test for you," or "You want to impress everyone, so here's your chance," or "Let's see you fall on your face with this one."

21. Forecast doom-and-gloom. Say things like, "When you foul this up, it's your hide," or "If this doesn't work, I'll have to re-evaluate your position."

How can the manager support the employee? The following steps clarify delegation and give the employee the support and trust needed. Here's what *to* do when delegating:

1. Give the employee work on important matters, not just make-work projects.

2. Don't exaggerate the importance of the delegation. It may simply be a one-shot task. If so, do not blow it out of proportion just to make the employee feel good. That's phony, and she'll know it.

3. Give the employee discretion over tasks and resources. Provide the information as to how and where to find various resources.

4. Set minimal guidelines early on. They should be clear, stated out-front, with checks and balances included. Then turn it over to the employee until time for reports or questions.

5. Make your uncertainties and apprehensions known, but do not smother.

6. Be consistent. Don't give a free-hand, then pull it back when things get uncomfortable.

7. Without overdoing, share your personal insights and experience. Delegation isn't a *stand-on-your-own* experience. Don't play a *it's your problem* game. You are there to lead; this means helping with uncertain situations in moments of indecision.

8. Don't be coy about sharing objective information and factual data.

9. Set specific times for reports. Do not ask questions in public or in front of others. Questions should be asked in private.

10. Help the employee develop options and alternatives. Two heads are almost always better at planning than one. When possible, different approaches should be explored; allow for new action and creative ideas to be tested.

11. Give the employee visibility and recognition both inside and outside the department. Build relationships and connections; help find ways to use delegation appropriately.

12. You may even find a mentor to help the employee further develop her or his judgment and savvy. Sooner or later properly-managed delegation leads to an accomplished goal or satisfactory progress. As the project continues, the necessity for attention may lessen or cease altogether.

Follow-through with the employee (on a strictly professional basis, of course) may continue. This is the task of the mentor. A mentor does some or all of these activities:

1. Takes face-to-face time to re-evaluate the employee's performance.

2. Listens to the employee's emotional reactions (if any) to the task.

3. Suggests ways to develop optional problem-solving approaches.

4. Plans the next project with the employee, with an eye to increasing complexity and responsibility.

5. Listens to the employee's apprehensions, then asks: "In what ways can we go about handling these feelings?" The mentor does some brief work-related (not psychological) counseling with the employee.

6. Assists the employee in finding an area of work in which he can become the recognized local expert.

7. Acknowledges resistance or objections raised in regard to #6.

8. Respects confidentiality at all times.

9. Does not play power games with the employee.

10. Does not try to coerce or surprise the employee; respects the employee's wishes about future work assignments.

11. Is willing to assume the role of mentor in the first place; does not start something which he later regrets and fails to see to its conclusion.

12. Uses the employee as a consultant and seeks feedback about ways the organization might improve service.

Finally, a caution: delegation is sometimes incorrectly interpreted as a reward rather than an acknowledgement of competence. The manager must always avoid the appearance of favoritism. Consequently, the manager will delegate solely on the basis of recognized merit and ability, not on the basis of emotions or personality. If a question about favoritism arises, the manager has several options: ignore it, reprimand the people who bring it up, or listen carefully to employee complaints and ask for specific examples of favoritism. Stay open-minded even if you don't agree.

Some employees compare compliments. Praise or delegation given to one employee might sometimes result in other employees feeling ignored, indirectly criticized, or even punished. This is especially true when employees consider themselves equally deserving, or are unaware of the co-worker's accomplishments and abilities.

Managers can avoid these potential conflicts by occasionally praising employees privately (when the praise is merited, of course) and reserving commendations or delegation for employees whose accomplishments are publicly recognized by everyone. Employee discontent and resentment are sticky to manage. Listening intently and telling employees the truth lessen the dangers to the manager. When the manager is truthful and trustworthy, employees have no need—and no basis—for accusations of favoritism.

Chapter 8

Feedback and Service: Staying on Track

Feedback is job-related communication between the employee and the manager. Feedback focuses on technical, work-oriented skills, relationships, and morale issues that affect performance.

Initiating and maintaining feedback is the primary leadership function of every manager. Feedback is the manager's essential tool for improving communication and performance, building effective work teams, reducing fear and distrust, and offering service to employees.

Here's a more comprehensive definition of feedback: a two-way communication about basic work information, mutually given and received, by both employees and managers, covering positive and negative performance, with predetermined guidelines and expectations; there should be no surprises.

Let's examine this definition in detail:

1. *Two-way communication of basic job-related information*: Feedback is not simply from the top-down, the employee can also initiate feedback. It's a two-way process, information flows back-and-forth between manager and employee. A feedback session usually occurs at an appointed time but may also occur spontaneously. Feedback may deal with a problem or a grievance, with ideas or questions, with feelings or apprehensions. It might

also occur when the manager has to resolve or prevent a problem. Feedback is sometimes used to correct mistakes and improve performance, but is never used to punish, get even, or humiliate. It's purpose is to keep people on the right track and reduce distrust. Motives are very important.

2. *Mutually given and received:* Feedback is a two-way communication, not one-way. It is a structured situation in which both parties, not just the manager, are free to give and receive information about their performance, to respond, to ask questions, or offer explanations. It is not an off-the-cuff conversation. Normally it's a scheduled routine in the work cycle.

3. *About employee and management performance:* Its purpose is to increase productivity by handling technical problems and work relationships. Feedback does not strictly deal with psychological matters such as marriage or family conflicts. However, work-related issues often have psychological dimensions such as tardiness or drinking on the job. Even though the manager is not a professional counselor, he can still listen and advise about behavior and emotions which eventually have an effect on the troubled employee's morale, productivity and performance. However, if these emotional problems are lingering and intrusive, the manager ought to refer the employee to a professional counselor with the knowledge and confidential assistance of the employer.

In fact, feedback should always be considered highly confidential, particularly by the manager, even if it involves common knowledge. The topics may not seem sensitive on the surface but people's emotions and reputations are nonetheless involved. It is always risky for a manager to discount an employee's right to privacy, regardless of the topic.

4. *About positive and negative performance.* The manager's feedback is intended to provide support to the employee. It deals with what's right in the organization, as well as what's wrong. It is the manager's way of acknowledging an employee's effectiveness and

contribution to a job well done. The manager never exaggerates or manufactures positive feedback, however. This is artificial, it demeans both parties and compromises credibility.

5. *With specific guidelines.* Guidelines ought to be known by everyone and clearly announced well in advance. Here are the main guidelines for effective feedback:

- It is a routine, normal management procedure and is not invoked only as a crisis response.

- Every employee is regularly involved in the feedback process.

- It is regularly scheduled, once a month for example. The times can also be publicly posted. This legitimizes the process in everyone's eyes.

- Appointments are scheduled at least two weeks in advance. However, the manager is also available at the employee's request.

- Timing is important; sessions should be scheduled when people are not hurried.

- Negative feedback takes one item at a time, not a whole list of issues.

- It covers recent events or current issues, not old, stale material.

- It is helpful, not punitive.

- Both parties avoid accusations, attributing motives, guesswork and psychoanalyzing.

- The sessions deal with facts and behavior related to morale and professional performance, not with prejudicial likes and dislikes.

- It is more positive than negative; good performance is always included.

- It occurs in a private, out-of-the-way location, not in a public place.

- It need not last more than fifteen or thirty minutes, unless the issues open further discussion.

- It may take twelve to twenty-four months for employees to accept it as routine.

- The manager must be consistent and patient as employees try feed back.

- The manager must guarantee confidentiality unless the information involves risk to life, property or health.

- If action is ever taken as a result of feedback information, the source of the information must be protected if at all possible.

When specific goals are decided, it is often useful to provide the employee with a dated and written summary of the session describing the agreed-upon expectations, goals and time lines involved.

If an ultimatum is involved, this exceeds the intentions of feedback. In this situation, it is wise to document the session. If someone's job or reputation is involved, the ultimatum is best given with witnesses present who represent both management and employees.

Some employees may at first be suspicious, reluctant, incredulous or even hostile to the manager's initial feedback attempts. The manager may have to avoid the temptation to give up and retaliate out of ego, anger or resentment. Some reasons why employees may resist the feedback process include:

1. Some aggressive employees are resistant to authority; they may fight for control or dominance.

2. Some cautious, withdrawn employees might respond only with grunts or one-syllable answers.

3. Feedback requires some degree of openness. But some employees are defensive, fearful or apologetic. These employees may deflate the process; try to ignore or minimize this potential problem.

4. There are recognition-seekers in every group who use feedback only to blow their own horn.

5. When it gets too close to home, some employees will call attention to side issues as a way of distracting the conversation.

6. Some immature employees may be coy and cute.

7. Militant workers sometimes use feedback as a soapbox for gripes or grievances.

8. Some nit-picking employees focus on insignificant details, rattling on about minor factors and highlighting personal biases.

9. Some uptight employees use feedback as a confessional, a way to rehash old material or an opportunity to clean their slate about past mistakes.

10. There are employees who enjoy telling secrets. They're not genuine *whistleblowers* trying to save money or prevent abuse. They're just loudmouths who'll reveal what other employees have done or said; either for spite or to gain attention.

How does the manager begin to implement a feedback program on a regular basis? Here are major factors to be considered:

Feedback factor #1: Readiness. How ready for regular feedback is the manager? How ready are employees? Each person has a different degree of receptivity or readiness for feedback. In the early stages feedback can look and sound threatening.

The manager has responsibility for initiating the feedback process. He also must be aware of the need for individual differences. It is critical that he monitor each employee's legitimate apprehensions. How? Ask! Get feedback about feedback. The manager must also remember that each employee will have a different pace and tolerance for feedback. That's why employees must be treated similarly but singularly. The manager cannot compare or comment upon someone else's style or speed. Patience and support are absolutely critical.

Feedback factor #2: Actively listening. The most basic feedback skill for the manager is active listening. To gain credibility in the work community the manager cannot be naive or uninformed about what goes on in it. To learn what employees think and believe the manager has to gain credibility. To do so, one indispensable listening skill stands out: intensive, non-interruptive listening. This type of listening is central to a manager's credibility. It is called *intensive* because concentration and unwavering attention are emotionally draining and physically demanding. Try listening with your body and mind for five to ten minutes, keeping your eyes and ears focused solely upon the speaker, without looking over his shoulder or fiddling with some object. Keep your focus on the other person and disregard your own feelings. Maintaining intense, riveted, unwavering interest is indeed a demanding enterprise.

It's called *non-interruptive* listening because, at some point in every conversation, each one of us wants to say something—usually before the other person is really finished. We want to be heard and interrupting is the usual strategy. But when a manager interrupts an employee, the danger is that the employee will feel the manager is exercising, possibly abusing, power. He'll assume that, by interrupting, the manager is really saying, "I don't want to hear what you're saying, so I'll take over now." The employee will be guarded and reluctant to try again.

Try listening for five minutes to someone with whom you disagree or to whom you are not particularly drawn. Don't interrupt or correct them. Don't barge in or display impatience. Don't rush them or mutter under your breath. You'll quickly see that it is very difficult to maintain intense and undivided attention without interrupting, especially when you are bursting to explain, clarify or defend a point.

Feedback factor #3: Employee's perceptions. Intensive, non-interruptive listening is the key to understanding the employee's perceptions; i.e., how the employee sees and interprets his work experiences. The employee's words reveal powerful, intimate (and not always pleasant) perceptions. The effective manager becomes familiar with the employee's perceptions, no matter how different or unsavory they may be. The manager will listen intently, uncritically and constructively, without interrupting, challenging, or defending, until she understands the employee's words and his deeper meaning and emotions. Of course, the manager may not agree with everything she hears, but she needs to hear it nonetheless.

Feedback factor #4: Building trust. Active listening nurtures trust with employees. Active listening also increases the employee's sense of inclusion and equality. It says in effect that the employee is valued and respected. Some ways in which the manager increases credibility include:

1. Using employees as consultants, asking their advice or opinions.

2. Asking about the employee's perceptions. It is legitimate to ask questions about outlook, but be careful about asking off-the-wall questions, introducing a whole new avenue of discussion, asking intrusive, nosy questions, nit-picking, pushing too far, or threatening the employee.

3. Volunteering management information, or data which the employee may not have.

4. Sharing management information which has influenced your feelings and viewpoints in the past.

5. Helping the employee develop options and new alternatives. Two heads are better at planning than one.

Feedback factor #5: Most important skills. In the long run, telling the truth, being honest, and listening intently and supportively are the best ways the manager can express positive appreciation, recognition and inclusion. Being honest and listening carefully without interruption are the heart and soul of feedback, the invaluable arts in building credible relationships.

Chapter 9

Rules of Professionalism in Sales

We can identify three phases in sales: Preparation, Accommodation, and Insight. Each phase has certain rules connected to it as follows:

Phase 1: Preparation: Understanding basic sales principles.

Rule #1. The salesperson's first role is service. The goal is to meet a need as well as to make a sale. The seller offers service but is not a servant. Civility, not servility, is appropriate. Courtesy, not a hard-sell, is the norm. The first thirty seconds with the customer are usually the most significant for setting the salesperson's tone and style. For example, will the salesperson be jovial or serious with this customer? Will the customer set the pace of the conversation, or will the salesperson keep control of the conversation? Whatever the goal, service is the foremost role.

Rule #2. The customer's concerns always come first—always. Buyers are sometimes arrogant and hostile, unavailable and aloof. That's fine. The inexperienced or fatigued salesperson might take the snubs personally, and that's *not* fine. The salesperson may have to swallow feelings and curtail impulses. He or she must not show a dislike for the customer, be defensive, flippant, dogmatic or stern (unless things get out of hand). Working with customers can be unpleasant, but that's part of the job.

As a rule, no matter how the buyer behaves the salesperson maintains professional demeanor and a service mentality. Even legitimate *off-the-wall* questions or requests deserve attention. The customer's concerns are paramount.

If the customer is insulting or hard to handle, the salesperson need not grin-and-bear-it. No one is required to tolerate abuse or harassment when the customer is clearly out of order. But the sales rule requires that the salesperson does not retaliate with insulting or unpleasant behavior. The only recourse is to be emphatic and assertive.

Rule #3. Immediate sales are not the only goal of selling. The success of most businesses depends on the repeat customer. This means viewing sales from a long-term perspective. Developing an extended relationship with a customer means earning a place in the customer's buying routine, meriting referrals, converting the buyer into a missionary for your business.

The long-term questions are: How can the salesperson change the occasional browser into a regular? How can the customer be impressed with the salesperson's willingness to serve as well as sell? How is it possible to become a consultant and problem-solver in the customer's mind?

Rule #4. Trying to persuade the customer to buy is far less effective than forging a personal relationship. Trying to persuade a customer always skirts the possibility of raising defenses, starting an argument, forcing resistance, or even refusal. It's always unwise to introduce a negative into the sales relationship. New buyers are particularly prone to resist sales overtures; they are attuned to the ancient adage "caveat, emptor," buyer, beware. The seller's credibility is the best sales tactic.

Phase 2: Accommodation: Understanding the nuances of service.

Rule #5. Seek the customer's comfort. Each customer requires a degree of physical space before being at ease. It's a highly personal zone that affords physical comfort and emotional security. This space is protected, especially from unknown personalities such as a new salesperson. It can be shared to varying degrees, according to the stranger's attractiveness or how useful the new person can be in reaching a goal. If a salesperson suddenly intrudes upon a customer's private zone, it will be instinctively defended or the customer will back away. Most people do not militantly stand their ground unless there is a reason, so in a sales context the customer will simply leave.

The salesperson can violate the customer's comfort zone in a number of ways: physical touching without reason, speaking too loud or often, moving too quickly, standing too close, grabbing an item from the customer, being too nosy, familiar or arbitrary.

Respecting the customer's comfort is best done by teaching salespeople to ask themselves, "How would I feel if I were treated as I am treating this customer?"

Rule #6. Do not aggravate or antagonize the customer. Most are patient and reasonable, but each has a limit beyond which he or she will not go. Avoid the customer's threshold of aggravation. Once the threshold is crossed, there's little chance of recovery. That is when the customer will most likely say "Let me speak to the Manager," or simply vanish, never to be seen again. But know for sure that the customer will be *heard* time and time again with a juicy anecdote about how bad your service is. You can bet that the story will be repeated as often as the opportunity presents itself.

Sometimes crossing the threshold of anger may take a customer many months. Other times it may take only a minute. A customer does not cross the threshold arbitrarily; there are always reasons. The most frequent reasons are feeling ignored, waiting too long, and faults or errors in the merchandise.

As the customer nears his threshold he will sound and look increasingly agitated and impatient. If the salesperson is attentive, there's no way an upset or troubled customer can be missed. The customer will announce his moods.

Rule #7. It's what the customer thinks, not what the seller intends, that counts. It's the salesperson's attention, not intention, that matters. If the salesperson avoids or ignores the customer a problem exists. Even if the salesperson is busy, the buyer must receive some sign of recognition. Once they meet, the customer deserves the salesperson's undivided listening attention and concentration. Distractions and work demands will occasionally intrude, employees cannot control external factors but they can control their reactions to them.

Rule #8. The seller must never complain to the customer. The employee never troubles the customer with gripes and problems (particularly work problems). Customers are not part-time therapists; they do not want to hear the salesperson's gripes. Gossip about work or other customers is totally out of order.

Rule #9. The customer always has a right. The sales situation involves an implicit agreement between buyer and seller in which roles are clear and their relationship is defined. The buyer is placed in a dependent position in the seller's world because he or she is looking for something. It is the seller's obligation to help find it. Customer service depends on the buyer and seller honoring these norms. If they insensitively intrude on one another's egos, they will become defensive. An adversarial situation arises in which courtesy and good-will are violated. The sales experience will be distressing to both parties and no goals will be accomplished. For their mutual benefit, hostility and conflict are to be avoided and good will and courtesy honored.

It is ultimately the seller's—thus the manager's—responsibility to uphold these norms, to respect the customer's dignity, to make the sales experience as satisfying as possible. This holds true even when the customer does not honor his side of the contract. The service mentality says that customer's always have rights. Observing those rights is what makes a salesperson a professional.

Phase 3: Insight: Understanding the immediate sales scene.

Four factors influence the effectiveness of the sales situation: (1) The focus of the discussion that the seller must monitor, (2) How the seller manages time during the sales encounter, (3) The seller's staying power over time, and (4) The seller's listening ability.

Rule #10. The seller monitors the focus of the conversation. The focus of the discussion indicates how seriously the buyer takes the salesperson at the moment. It's up to the salesperson to stay with the topic or to bring the customer back if the conversation wanders. As a rule, the customer who rambles is not too concerned about the seller's time or product. The meandering buyer indicates the seller's usefulness is minimal. There is no urgency about buying, the product and the salesperson are apparently low priorities.

Too often a salesperson will hang-in, hoping the buyer will suddenly whip out a credit card as a reward for the seller's patience. This happens rarely. The more chit-chat the salesperson allows and encourages, the more unproductive the dialogue becomes.

Rule #11. The salesperson should watch the amount of time spent with each customer. She must be aware of what is happening as time passes during the sales encounter. It is important to learn what is productive and what is not, to carefully manage time. How much small talk is constructive? How long should the seller allow the buyer to wander? Does the buyer expect the salesperson to simply hang around during interruptions? Does the buyer take calls and expect the seller to wait passively? How long should the seller wait? Does the buyer ask lots of extraneous questions which could lead into time-consuming but fruitless discussions? The salesperson must remain attentive, but the only restriction on the buyer is a personal sense of courtesy.

Managing the time factor means the salesperson makes the decision to back off and return another day, to move on and find a customer more disposed to sales. When is the right time to leave? When can a courteous withdrawal be made without giving offense? How can the salesperson know that a sale has not been lost?

As a rule, the more time spent trying to seduce or win the customer's good will, the less won the customer will be. The more time spent in idle chit-chat and small talk, the less likely a sale will result. If more sales-focused customers are available, the best advice is: "Go get 'em!"

Rule #12. Persevere—but takes steps to handle discouragement. Perseverance means sticking with selling despite apparent rejections. The customer may appear unavailable or hostile, but it is almost always never personal. A *no sale* is simply a customer's decision not to buy; it's not a critical judgment or a rejection of the seller. It's not to be taken personally.

Nevertheless, the obvious problem in sales is lack of them. A series of *no sale* decisions can seem like a huge rejection, and burden the salesperson with a sense of hopelessness and a feeling of uselessness. After a time, the salesperson translates lack of sales into a negative self-judgment. He whips himself, he's no good as a salesperson, he'll never succeed. His self-esteem is shaken. He starts feeling like a loser. Without some kind of personal support system, the salesperson may become seriously depressed and physically ill. Perseverance is essential but the toll it takes must be counterbalanced by healthy and rewarding experiences in the salesperson's life.

Rule #13. A salesperson must see and hear what she listens to. Listening with customers is not a static, predictable process. Various situations call for different perspectives. Most people tend to listen and respond the same way under most circumstances. People change reluctantly only when compelled, for example, by another's anger, by a threat to the status quo (such as a divorce), or by an outside authority (a police officer giving a ticket for speeding).

Body language and voice intonations convey meaning in an indirect but very significant manner. Gestures are generally more accurate than words. In fact gestures often contradict what words state. They help to discriminate the customer's real intentions. Does he really like the product or do his averted eyes tell the salesperson a different story?

Here's a snippet of conversation illustrating how utterly ineffectual and unsettling some communication can be.

Diner: "I'll have steak medium rare, baked potato,
        Thousand Island . . ."

Waiter: "Sour cream or chives?"

Diner: "Ah. . . . Thousand Island . . ."

Waiter: "On the potato?"

Diner: "What? No, the salad . . ."

Waiter: "It's extra. . . ."

Diner: "The Thousand Island?"

Waiter: "No . . . the baked potato . . ."

Diner: "I'll have it anyway . . ."

Waiter: "The sour cream or the chives?"

Diner: "Let me change that."

Waiter: "The baked potato?"

Diner: "Let me have the prime rib . . ."

Waiter: "Would you like sour cream or chives?"

Diner: "Both."

Waiter: "It's extra . . ."

Diner: "The sour cream or the chives?"

Waiter: "The baked potato. . . . It's extra . . ."

Diner: "How's the halibut today?"

Waiter: "Fine. How would you like that done?"

Diner: "The prime rib?"

Waiter: "No, the halibut?"

Diner: "The halibut?"

Waiter: "Is that what you want?"

Diner: "Medium rare will be fine."

Waiter: "Thank you, sir."

Rule #14. Let the customer lead the sales discussion until it is no longer productive. Most sales conversations are like a tennis match; verbal control bounces from one person to another. Problems arise when both parties compete for control at the same moment. As a rule, when the customer wants control, let him have it until it is clear that he has no intention of staying with the sales topic. Then it is time to gently take over, re-direct the discussion to sales—or leave. Tell the customer you will be happy to help and available when he is ready.

Rule #15. Always give more than the customer expects. Over the past decade service has deteriorated in many professions. Most customers don't expect much from salespeople or businesses anymore. Customer complaints often go unheeded. The doctor who made house calls is long-gone. The gas station attendant who filled your tank and wiped your windshield is a thing of the past. Courtesy and personal attention are obsolete in many businesses.

That's why customers are pleasantly shocked and delighted when a salesperson seems to care enough to see that things are done correctly, someone who will take time to listen and please the buyer. That's how a business that sells from the buyer's point of view can stand above the competition. As an investment in customer relations, the generous service of a thoughtful salesperson costs the business nothing. But the return on that investment can be extraordinary in terms of repeat customers, long-term business relationships, referrals and a superior reputation for service.

Chapter 10

Self-Defeating Practices in Sales

Products don't always sell themselves. The salesperson is often the critical element in the customer's buying decisions. Some salespeople go to extraordinary lengths to please customers, delivering a purchase on their own time, paying the difference when the customer has insufficient cash, calling a competitor to locate a product. These deeds are obviously above and beyond the call of duty, but it's well-worth the effort to impress the customer with trouble-free service. Customers are more accustomed to conflict and disturbing events than pleasant ones; unexpected courtesies will happily overshadow the customer's apprehensions.

Careful, generous service produces four benefits: (1) It prevents horror stories that can ruin reputations, kill referrals, and turn customers away; (2) It establishes a distinct, attractive image in the customer's mind and produces good feelings; (3) Inasmuch as the customer has been given proof of genuine concern, it gives her a chance to return the *favor* by making referrals; and (4) Since many customers like to talk about new and noteworthy trends, the business receives free advertising when customers speak well of the service they have received. Incidentally, this is how customer service myths get started; it's the way a business can become a local legend in a relatively short time.

Although each transaction is a *moment of truth*, some employees never seem to understand their importance in the overall sales enterprise. They say,

"What difference does one customer make? Some customers are touchy; you can't please everyone, so why worry, right?" Wrong! This is a dangerous, short-sighted attitude that obviously must be corrected immediately and monitored at all costs. It's the cornerstone of the major self-defeating practices in sales and customer service.

Most sales managers and representatives, retail stores and manufacturers understate or totally deny how serious customer dissatisfaction really is. When the salesperson commits one of the following transgressions during the *moment of truth*, you might as well send the customer to the competition.

The major self-defeating practices in sales are abruptness, inappropriate familiarity, ignoring or avoiding the customer, bad hygiene, arguing with customers, and indifference (the *take-it-or-leave-it* attitude). These practices are indeed deadly to a business' sales and reputation. While most customers are tolerant, tolerance should never be expected. If you wish to keep customers coming back, give them a reason. These examples—as obviously ridiculous and avoidable as they are—expand on the above self-defeating practices and tell why so many businesses do not last.

1. Abruptness with Customers.

What is a customer to do with the abrupt salesperson or food server who:

- greets the customer with a gruff, perfunctory, "Yeah," or
- abruptly walks away when the customer is speaking, or
- is gruff, sullen, impatient or hostile, or
- drums his fingers and looks around distractedly while the customer is talking, or
- has all the answers before she hears the questions, or
- continually interrupts and never lets the customer finish a sentence, or
- tells the customer what to buy and—without being asked for an opinion—contradicts the customer's preference, or
- snarls when answering the phone, snaps at the caller, or puts the phone on hold without explanation, or

- cuts the customer off in mid-sentence because she believes she knows just what the customer needs?

Abrupt salespeople send a clear message to the customer: *You are an intrusion; you are not welcome!* The customer won't overlook barely tolerable behavior, particularly when competition is just a few doors or a phone call away. In these cases, the the only loser is the business that allows such behavior.

2. Inappropriate Familiarity.

Familiarity can be touchy, and the customer must never be taken for granted in this regard. A salesperson will never favorably impress a customer with a chummy or presumptuous approach. The customer may not say anything, but she'll remember how offensive and off-base the salesperson was. Most customers do not complain; more often they'll be courteous and pleasant, then they'll leave.

What is a customer to do with the salesperson who:

- is an instant backslapper and elbow-grabber, or

- winks and nudges the customer like an old buddy, or

- immediately works on a first-name basis, or

- calls people "Dearie" or "Hon" or "Pal". or

- insists on telling ethnic or off-color jokes as *ice-breakers*, or

- dresses in an embarrassingly revealing manner, or

- oozes oily enthusiasm and nauseating good will, or

- gossips personally with the customer about work conflicts?

3. Ignoring or Avoiding the Customer

The salesperson who ignores a customer or keeps her waiting without reason is playing with fire. When the customer is ignored the ego is threatened and anger is often the result.

What is a customer to do with the salesperson who:

- speaks in monosyllables, sighs, grunts, mumbles, or

- does not make eye contact or, worse, looks over the customer's shoulder, smiles and waves at someone else while the customer is talking, or

- continues to read a magazine while the customer waits, or

- never answers a direct question, or

- does not answer phone calls or letters, or

- makes the customer wait and wait and wait, or

- showers attention on one customer, then slights another?

4. Bad Hygiene

Television is filled with commercials for soap, tooth paste and hair spray. Why, then, are so many salespeople (and in some cases managers) still grubby and unkempt?

What is a customer to do about a salesperson or food server:

- whose work area is cluttered and filthy?

- who clearly needs a deodorant, a bath and a shave?

- whose breath would stagger a musk ox?

- whose fingernails need cleaning?

- who makes change, then serves food with his bare hands?

5. Arguing with Customers.

Some salespeople are constantly loaded for bear. Should a customer ask the wrong question or make a critical comment, the wrath comes tumbling out.

In such cases, what is a customer to do about the salesperson who:

- treats the customer like an unwelcome intruder, or

- takes each complaint as a personal offense, or

- is argumentative and defensive, or

- insists that, "We are not responsible" or "That's not our policy," or

- has an excuse for everything, or

- believes the customer has no rights?

6. Indifference, the *Take-it-or-Leave-It* Attitude

The blase salesperson acts as though he is doing the customer a favor. He fills the air with a cloud of indifference. The manager of the coffee shop in Chapter One is an example.

What is a customer to do with the salesperson who:

- exudes contempt, or

- is passive and uninvolved, or

- is constantly rushed and has no time for a customer, or

- says "No exceptions; take it as is, or not at all!" or

- is unwilling to help customers get what they really want, or

- reveals an attitude of unconcern for the customer, or

- answers the customer's questions with a shrug of the shoulders?

If any of these examples remind managers of an employee, better reread the chapter on feedback, or give that employee walking papers—quick!

Chapter 11

Customer Service Skills in Action

Superior customer service depends on many factors:

- The setting in which business occurs;
- The nature of the contact with the customer;
- The duration of contact with the customer;
- The frequency of contact with the same customer;
- Management expectations and philosophy of service;
- The level of employee's training;
- How the manager treats employees;
- Is emphasis on profit or customer service?

No single customer service skill fits all businesses, but several are necessary to create the proper environment. Those skills are: (1) Empathy, (2) Emotional Balance, (3) Responsiveness, (4) Observing the Obvious, (5) Timing, (6) Managing Information, and (7) Generosity, Going the Extra Mile. It is the manager's job to see that these skills are maintained.

1. The Skill of Empathy

Empathy is central to selling from the buyer's point of view. It means looking at each sales opportunity from the buyer's perspective. Empathy means listening to and meeting the customer's needs. It means temporarily forgetting personal needs while looking at the sales situation from the customer's standpoint. Empathy is the heart of selling from the buyer's point of view.

Empathy requires the salesperson to reserve judgment and give the customer every benefit of the doubt. Is the customer indecisive? Empathy dictates patience and self-control. Is the customer aggressive or cynical? Empathy cautions acceptance and open-minded attention. Is the customer contradictory or aloof? Empathy suggests a low-key approach.

Empathy prompts the salesperson to ask, "How would I feel if someone treated me the way I am treating this customer? Would I prefer to be rushed or ignored? Or, would I prefer to be given attention and courtesy even when I'm indecisive and distant?" Empathy is at the heart of the service mentality—giving more than asked, taking less than allowed.

2. Emotional Balance

This skill permits the salesperson to control his or her emotions, no matter what the circumstance. The service mentality dictates no temper tantrums or moodiness from salespeople, no loud or explosive laughter, no impatient or angry behavior, no arrogance or haughtiness. Emotional balance also warns the seller not to take each negative encounter to heart. Even if things go wrong, the salesperson must still mask his disappointment or hostility lest he make the buyer anxious or defensive.

First impressions are critical in the sales encounter. The salesperson is the buyer's first contact with a business. It's during those first thirty seconds—maybe less—that many sales are lost and reputations tarnished, simply because the salesperson was having a *bad day*. When it comes to the service mentality there is no such thing as a bad day; there is only bad service.

3. Responsiveness

Basic to the service mentality is prompt, courteous, consistent, and precise attention. There are several thoughtless acts that can aggravate customers and make them feel unwelcome. Here are several examples: the salesperson leisurely finishes a phone call even though she knows the customer is waiting. The salesperson continues filing her nails while the customer prowls around looking for someone to take his money. The skill of responsiveness is the salesperson's awareness that the convenience of the customer is part of the job. Unless there is a very good reason, a customer should never be kept waiting.

Responsiveness is single-minded and thorough. A responsive salesperson is noticeably focused and intensely attentive while the customer is speaking. This doesn't mean staring down the customer's throat. It does mean blocking all distractions and outside interests for the sake of serving the customer at that moment.

4. Observing the Obvious

This simply means the salesperson notices the customer's immediate need and tries to attend to that need at once. Some simple examples: filling an empty water glass, taking a customer's coat, calling a cab for the customer, holding a door open, or helping with packages and setting them down close by. Observing the obvious also involves taking internal initiative. For example, is inventory low? Do all the lights work? How about answering the phone? Does the parking lot need sweeping? Who puts unsold merchandise back on the shelf? There are endless housekeeping details that require attention and these also come under the heading of observing the obvious.

In daily business, observing the obvious means that the employee has the best interests of the business in mind. It is not necessary that the manager continuously tell her what to do. It is obvious what needs doing, so she does it.

5. Timing.

By the time a customer has to ask for service, he is already aggravated. The following are some of the things that cause this to happen:

- The customer has to wait in line for service even though there are unattended windows and employees are standing around talking to each other.

- The customer is put on telephone hold and no one comes back to say what is happening.

- The customer arrives on time at a restaurant to learn, despite a firm reservation, that there is a forty-five minute wait.

From another perspective, a salesperson may find the client so harried and distracted that his sales call is untimely. The best move is to say a quick, friendly goodbye, and leave quietly. Don't waste time hoping the client will be able to break free.

6. Managing Information.

When managers restrict the flow of information they create data gaps. Employees tend to fill gaps with hearsay, innuendo and gossip. They also attach negative motives to the manager who withholds data. It is good management practice to keep employees informed and included. Uninformed workers feel like outsiders; their interest and commitment wanes. Customers will notice, service will falter. It is better if the manager errs on the side of too much, rather than too little information.

There are several types of job-related information to which all employees should have access:

- Basic technical information: how to do routine tasks such as work the cash register or complete sales slips, where specific items are stored, how the telephone should be answered, where the utilities are located, how to keep inventory, etc.

- The manager's personal expectations: local customs and procedures, how the manager wishes customers to be greeted, how to handle complaints, the manager's policies on refunds or substitutions, local dress codes and styles, etc.

- Morale factors: decisions that influence the manager's credibility, ways to help employees with work problems, advancement and training, feedback schedules and guidelines, overtime opportunities, openings in the company, criteria for performance evaluations, salary increases and promotions, etc.

7. Generosity: Going the Extra Mile to give that Personal Touch.

Quality service means *the personal touch*. This includes attention to the customer's choices and accuracy in presenting those choices. In some businesses, the customer is used as a service consultant; he is periodically asked how the business could be more effective. Personal phone calls to the customer are impressive; not always necessary but still psychologically valuable. A customer may not always notice each personal touch but he will notice its absence.

Generosity means going the extra mile, giving more than asked, doing more than expected. Most businesses offer about the same products and services. If you've flown one airline you've flown them all. Clothing stores are pretty much alike. If you've tried one ethnic restaurant, you know what to expect elsewhere. Still, many customers have preferences. They stick with a favorite restaurant or store, a particular bank or doctor. Ask why and they'll often say it's the extra time and attention they receive. They have a sense of receiving something special, something personal, over-and-above what's expected.

In fact, generous salespeople really give something of themselves: sincere courtesy, genuine concern, appropriate laughter, warm and personal greetings that ring true. Going the extra mile means making a point to remember the client's name, projecting a sense of welcome that goes beyond the consumer's expectations. That's what makes the difference. It is often enough to make the difference between a business that just breaks even, and one that soon becomes a familiar household name.

Of course, generosity is not always a matter of altruism or self-sacrifice. It makes good business sense to outshine the competition in whatever way possible. Every experienced manager knows that most products do not differ significantly. So, in the long run, effective sales come down to the credibility and authenticity of the salespeople.

From the buyer's point of view it's the generosity of the salesperson and the quality of his manager that adds luster and zest to the sales endeavor.

Chapter 12

Staying Healthy When It All Catches Up to You

The ceaseless and stressful demands on the manager inevitably take a toll. With time, she or he may feel more and more depressed or listless, gloomy or cynical, sad or powerless. If these feelings last for more than a few days they may be the early signs of serious burnout.

Burnout is a state of physical, mental, emotional and spiritual exhaustion. Burnout results from too few positives and too many negatives, from too little support or acknowledgement and too many uninterrupted pressures. The burned out manager becomes plagued by exhaustion, low energy, and fatigue. Various ailments such as back tension, unexplained nausea, and a number of psychosomatic complaints are often experienced.

Mental exhaustion is part of this situation. Interest wanes and a sense of alienation emerges. Negative attitudes develop toward work, salespeople and customers. Feelings of incompetence and inadequacy arise. Emotional exhaustion also occurs and motivation decreases. People suffering from burnout experience depression, irritability, nervousness, feelings of helplessness, hopelessness, and increasing isolation.

Burnout is a form of long-term stress. It doesn't happen overnight. It occurs gradually over a period of months, even years. No one, no matter how highly motivated or sincere, is immune. Dedication cannot prevent burnout.

In fact, highly idealistic, well-motivated people are often the most severely afflicted. The manager might be able to mask stress and burnout symptoms for a time, but unrelieved stress will still pursue its dangerous and silent course toward eventual burnout.

Burnout can be very sneaky. Most people fall into burnout while still doing their jobs. The greatest danger is not a major crisis or catastrophe. Nature has equipped us to handle heavy, demanding events; we are always aware of the pain and cost associated with a crisis. The big danger is the gradual erosion of our physical energy and emotional resources. We adjust to tension and anxiety almost imperceptibly. We gradually accept them as normal when indeed they are not. Thus, it's the cumulative affect of commonplace drudgery and unrewarding endeavors, of mounting tedium and loss of purpose that drain commitment, motivation, and zeal.

There are three stages in the burnout process. The first stage is called the *Alarm Reaction*. When new or unusual stress occurs, our body exhibits definite reactions. These include an increase in blood pressure and heart rate, sweating, changes in breathing, alterations in the immune system. The ability to handle more stress is decreased.

The second is the *Stage of Resistance*. If the stress becomes chronic (continuous), not just acute (short-term), the body begins to adapt. These pressures are accepted as normal when they're highly abnormal, and the individual is still not aware of the price being paid.

The final stage is the *Stage of Exhaustion*. After a time, the person becomes exhausted, adaptive energy is used up, and resources are gone. Burnout occurs. Everything begins to noticeably fall apart. Work degenerates, relationships crack at the seams. Bizarre behaviors often sprout up; heavy drinking is not uncommon. Grooming and attire may become careless and sloppy, meetings and deadlines are missed, and sarcastic and cynical remarks may be heard. Clearly something is seriously wrong; it's apparent to everyone except the sufferer. He or she is often unaware of how dramatic and disturbing these changes are.

How long does it take to reach burnout? That depends on several factors: physical health, leisure habits and work schedule, constitution and mental outlook, support systems, and common sense.

What can a person do to prevent or overcome burnout? There are many effective ways; here are a few.

1. Get regular exercise; develop a physical outlet for your energy. Many medical experts believe that exercise is the single best way to prevent chronic stress and avoid burnout. Clinical research demonstrates that regular exercise is effective in combatting depression and cardiovascular disease. However, if you have not exercised since school, are out of shape, or are uncertain how to begin exercising, consult a physician before beginning any exercise program. Don't let ego eclipse common sense.

2. Use your head and be honest about symptoms. Do not ignore the early signs of burnout. Don't try to convince yourself they'll go away. A busy schedule is no excuse and can actually make matters worse. We all feel listless and discouraged at times, that's normal; but if these symptoms persist beyond several days, it's time to pay attention and face facts.

3. Watch out for ego. Aggressive people are particularly prone to denying a problem. *I can handle anything*, is the common myth. Many are convinced that they are so vital and important that they must do everything and be responsible for everyone. Isolated self-importance is purely and simply an ego problem. It's also a sign of burnout vulnerability because it encourages rationalization and toleration of greater levels of discomfort in the name of dedication.

4. Seek out emotional support from someone you trust. Reveal your feelings and concerns to a loved one or a close friend on a regular basis. Some degree of intimacy is essential for everyone's emotional balance. Handling feelings and moods, especially negative ones, is a basic requirement for a healthy, well-balanced personality.

5. Avoid the wrong solutions. Addictive chemicals like nicotine, alcohol, and illegal drugs are not remedies. They cure nothing and often create more problems by tearing down the body's reserves and depleting physical energy.

Many organizations regularly serve alcohol as part of business rituals. This is highly suspect. Alcohol is not an appropriate addition to business dealings. It is a depressant that affects mood and health.

6.   Watch your diet. Our ability to handle normal stress depends first on our physical resiliency. Proper diet and nutrition play significant long-term roles in health. It's important (especially when traveling) to avoid heavy meals, fried foods, excessive sugar and salt, drugs and alcohol. In fact it's best to cut these items out of one's diet entirely.

7.   Don't punish yourself emotionally. Avoid self-criticism and dire predictions about the future. Don't try to convince yourself that you should be able to handle all problems alone. This thinking sparks many problems, and be careful about guilt. Useless, prolonged guilt is a frequent forerunner of burnout.

8.   Short-term counseling from a qualified professional may be useful. Certified professionals such as psychologists, social workers, pastoral, and mental health counselors can be found in the phone book. Ask your physician or pastor for a referral. Consult professional associations listed in the telephone book. Check your insurance. Many policies provide coverage for counseling.

When seeking counseling, don't hesitate to check out the counselor. Be sure he or she is certified by the appropriate health department in your state. Ask the counselor about his credentials, training and education, background and present professional affiliations. How much are the charges? How long are the counseling sessions? How many sessions are normal? Does the counselor help you express yourself freely and supportively? Are you at ease with the counselor or do you have reservations? Are questions answered directly? Is the counselor open and responsive about methods and procedures?

If you are unsure or ill at ease, try someone else. Remember: caveat, emptor! As a consumer you always have rights. You are paying for a service; you're entitled to know what—and who—you are paying for. You should know exactly what you and the counselor are doing. You should also know how the counselor can help you. Don't hesitate to ask direct questions and exercise your rights, especially with someone you're about to trust with highly confidential, personal material. If you are not satisfied with the answers, move on.

9.   Do something mentally or artistically stimulating on a regular basis. Try a class or a project you've delayed. Write poetry, listen to or play music. Whatever you choose, don't make it competitive or demanding. Use it as a leisure time, creative outlet, not a win-lose contest.

The old adage "Use it or lose it" truly applies to our mental processes, our creativity, and our memory. Using the brain is healthy, it helps us to maintain intellectual alacrity.

10.   Take quiet time in the morning and evening for yourself. In the early hours, focus on beginning each morning anew. Make each day an opportunity to pursue one small, personal goal. Use five minutes of silence first thing in the morning to focus your mind and resources on a positive accomplishment—something within your grasp—like doing an act of kindness. Keep your focus on today's target. Then proceed in a clearly-defined direction.

At night, scan the day in your memory. Reflect on the moments of accomplishment. Even when you're surrounded by problems, taking time to create inner calm is emotionally healthy.

11.   Face your fears directly and quickly. The best way through any intimidating experience is confronting its source as soon as possible, and with support when it's needed. We usually do not think of ourselves as courageous, but working through fear and intimidation—especially as it relates to burnout—may require truly heroic sacrifice and noble effort.

12.   Humor is psychologically healthy. Exploit laughter (not people) without forcing or falsifying it. Find the humorous or ridiculous

aspects of life. Laughter softens the serious edges and makes harsh events easier to bear. The magic chemistry of a smile alleviates immediate stress and is a long-term curative for burnout.

13. Relish love in your life. Of all emotions, love and trust are the best long-term antidotes to emotional loneliness. Let your loved ones express their caring and be open to physical expressions of affection. Accept love where it exists, extend it where it is lacking.

14. Learn more about stress and burnout. While burnout can be severe, it is always possible to bounce back. Books and seminars are readily available. Be choosy; examine the credentials of the so-called *experts*.

Finally, make time for self-examination and be honest with yourself. Is your work a source of continuing tension and anxiety? Is it leading toward a dark and dreary future? Are you less satisfied than you want to be? If your answers are yes, it's time to do something. Don't expect others to take responsibility for your choices. Friends and loved ones cannot do it for you. The more you look to others to define your value and worth, the less fulfillment you'll find; they're probably busy working on themselves. Your first responsibility is to maintain your own well-being. All peace of mind and healthy self-esteem flow from physical and emotional well-being.

Perhaps the greatest benefit of taking charge of your own life is the simple knowledge that you have accepted personal responsibility for yourself. That's how we define maturity. In the process, we can also learn a great deal about life's essential values and priorities.

You may have to work hard to manage stress and stay ahead of the costly twists and turns in business. It may be necessary to pursue life with unflagging good will, despite the apathy or indifference of others. You would be wise, then, to seek purpose and meaning each day, to combat cynicism and fuel idealism. Idealism is no longer a luxury, it's a requirement if you are to successfully and generously fulfill the service mandate of giving more than asked and taking less than allowed.

About the Author

Daniel M. Boland, Ph.D. has been a teacher, speaker, organizational consultant and psychologist for more than twenty-five years, and has degrees in philosophy, counseling and theology, and a doctorate in psychology. Dr. Boland taught at several major universities and has been a member of leading professional associations for three decades.

The author currently speaks and writes about the theory and practice of Generous Leadership, personal traits related to effective management behavior, and management's impact on organizational stress and burnout. In addition to *Let Me Speak to the Manager!*, Dr. Boland has written *If It Hurts, Do Something;* and *The Evolving Manager*, and has also written more than seventy original workbooks for his various seminars and presentations.

He presently writes, speaks and consults from his home base Arcata, California, in the heart of the Northern California redwood forest. He is available for seminars, speaking and consulting programs.